Praise for *Estates Sales Made Easy*

"If you're looking to start an estate sale business,
Estate Sales Made Easy is a go-to guide for all the how-tos you
need to have success. Along with practical advice, Victoria also
shares touching stories of interactions with family members—
those still here and those on the other side! When you finish
this book, you'll have a much better understanding of the head
and heart needed to handle such delicate events."

— **Kerri Richardson,** author of
What Your Clutter Is Trying to Tell You

"The stories and background that lead to Victoria Gray's career
and passion give *Estate Sales Made Easy* a more human side and
are an inspiration to a lot of people that may find themselves in
the same situation. Ms. Gray's step-by-step information in the
profession, eliminates a lot of trial by error so people with a desire
to take this path can reach their goals much faster, and have a
guide they can take anywhere for reference."

— **Bertha 'Bert' Kaslin,** real estate agent,
Coldwell Banker Gundaker

ESTATE SALES
Made Easy

ALSO BY VICTORIA GRAY

Victoria Zane: A Dream-Based Novella

The Secret of a Widow's Vision: The Vision from Within

Victoria Gray Unfolded: The Speaking Linens

The Ankle Express: Life and Times of Wm. Victor Gray

Victorian Journal Guide

ESTATE SALES
Made Easy

A PRACTICAL
GUIDE TO SUCCESS
FROM START TO FINISH

VICTORIA GRAY

HAY HOUSE, INC.
Carlsbad, California • New York City
London • Sydney • Johannesburg
Vancouver • New Delhi

Published and distributed in the United States by: Hay House, Inc.: www
.hayhouse.com® • *Published and distributed in Australia by:* Hay House
Australia Pty. Ltd.: www.hayhouse.com.au • *Published and distributed in the
United Kingdom by:* Hay House UK, Ltd.: www.hayhouse.co.uk • *Published
and distributed in the Republic of South Africa by:* Hay House SA (Pty), Ltd.:
www.hayhouse.co.za • *Distributed in Canada by:* Raincoast Books: www
.raincoast.com • *Published in India by:* Hay House Publishers India: www
.hayhouse.co.in

Cover design: Amy Rose Grigoriou • *Interior design:* Riann Bender
Interior photo credits: Jumeau doll on p. 107 courtesy of Turn of the Century
Antiques in Denver, Colorado, www.rare-dolls.com
All other images courtesy of Victoria Gray

Cataloging-in-Publication Data is on file at the Library of Congress

Tradepaper ISBN: 978-1-4019-5302-7

10 9 8 7 6 5 4 3 2 1
1st edition, August 2017

Printed in the United States of America

To my wonderful children . . .

Rachel ~ Caleb

Blake ~ Ashley

Thank you for choosing me as your mother!

Love,
Momma

CONTENTS

INTRODUCTION

From the time I was a small child, I've had an affinity for adventure. Probably because my father took our family on one-day car rides to his hometown several times each year, telling stories of his childhood along the way. I became accustomed to these ancestral treasure trove adventures and the wonderment it brought me. Dad, as the leader in the family, only exemplified kindness and generosity with his time and teachings, molding, if you will, his precious babies into the same. He encouraged me to see things in a different light, to take a different road than my peers, by enlightening me to the various aspects of the universe and all it holds within the sun and stars.

His vast kindness caused me to think of others and how I might help them for the greater good of one and all. This is why the estate sale business intrigued me so much. I could feed, clothe, and house my family while helping others at the same time with a task that had almost disabled them within their grief.

Each estate sale is an adventure in and of itself. Each home houses energies from those that resided within, whether the person lived there for a long or a short period of time. Some are pleasant, enjoyable, and just plain lovely! Some are filled with anger, irritation, and angst. As I enter each sale, I pay attention to all energy fields as to what I may receive, holding all thoughts inside so I can journal them when I return home.

I have to say, when I began to *feel* and *think* there was something more, something extraordinary from within, was at age 14—just after I was almost shocked to death.

One sweltering Tuesday in August 1966, it was my day to wash the lunch and dinner dishes. All the windows were open, and the huge attic fan and roll-about fan were on. The hot dish water combined with the almost unbearable August heat wave caused me to move the metal fan to blow more directly on me, and at the same time, reach with my right hand to open the kitchen drawer to drop in the hand-dried silverware. With both hands damp and both surfaces metal, I received a shock that took me to my knees.

I screamed, "Help me, help me!"

In my head, my scream was a miniscule scream; however, later on, neighbors three houses away stated they heard me yelling. My mother jumped out of the bath, dripping wet with a towel down her front, tripped over the cord that stretched from the other side of the kitchen to the fan, and disconnected the current, which could have killed her too. My brother ran inside to find me slumped on the floor.

Of course, I came through that scare. And just after this shocking experience, I began to hear inside my head what others were about to say before they spoke.

A few years before my first marriage, I worked at my aunt's home doing the books for her husband's very lucrative tree-trimming business. Aunt Katye, along with her sister, my mother, and family, came from very meager means and learned all about saving money and where to find great deals. Somewhere during my tenure there from age 15 to 17, she stated that she had bought some items at auctions, which helped stretch their growing budget. I'd never been introduced to auctions before or even knew what they were. Dear Aunt Katye soon thereafter drove to our home and took me to an auction in the country. I was amazed at the way it was handled. Lots of "yep, yep, yep" went on from the auctioneer. He stood at the podium rattling off names of items, asking for this amount or that amount, and eventually he'd say something sold. It was hard to understand what he said, and he ran so quickly that I didn't buy a thing.

Another pivot point came shortly after my second husband died without life insurance. I knew, as a mother of four, it was up to me to provide for my babies. Thus I began attending many seminars on business building and real estate buying, spending lots of time and money on learning tools for various business start-ups.

At one seminar on buying and selling bonds for cars, land, and houses via auctions, my ears perked up. I went to a few more business seminars, finding the auction business seminars most intriguing, and purchased all the information, enthusiastically reading and studying it when the patters of little feet were off in dreamland.

I also attended local high-end auctions to jot down notes as to what this or that sold for and to learn what the items were called, buying several books listing sold prices for antiques as well.

After about six months of gaining knowledge on the subject, I jumped into a new auction business.

Another crossroads happened during the fall of 1994, when I began noticing what seemed to be a whirling of invisible winds above my St. Louis home. I felt something was causing me to see things in an entirely different way than my upbringing via the family religion. I knew there was so much more to understand.

With the knowledge that something more was and is always needed, I feverishly read three to four books on business and/or metaphysics each week for 10 years, every morning before my little ones awoke.

A new business began and a new level of thinking emerged. I stepped out of my comfort zone, and the grand universe began to provide.

This book will guide you through beginning your own estate sale business with step-by-step instructions, plus along the way share bonus stories of seeing and feeling spiritual nuances.

Chapter One

GETTING
STARTED

STEP 1: Check out estate sales in your area to see *if* this truly interests you.[1]

    a. Check local estate sale companies online and their years in business; choose those with many years to research.

    b. Look online to compare local estate sales companies' percentage rates/fees and how they handle their sales. Also note past-sale links, if available, to view uploaded pictures. Pictures go a long way to entice the crowd of customers.

    STEP 2: Consult with professionals, such as an accountant, attorney, financial adviser, and other experts for advice regarding your small business.

    I went to **SCORE**[2], which is a nonprofit association dedicated to helping small businesses get off the ground, grow, and achieve their goals through education and mentorship. They've been doing this for over 50 years and can be found online.

STEP 3: Choose a business name.

- File a creation document with the secretary of state, if needed.

- Follow your state guidelines.

    Corporation—Articles of incorporation

    General Partnership—No creation document required, but fictitious name filing may be necessary

    Limited Partnership—Certificate of limited partnership

    Limited Liability Company—Articles of organization

- Consider fictitious name registration—If the business will operate under a name other than your own or the exact name of the spiritual being, you must register that different name.

- Sole Proprietorships—A sole proprietor is someone who owns an unincorporated business by himself or herself.

You can access many of these filings electronically through the secretary of state's online services.

STEP 4: Register the business for required state taxes, if applicable. Speak to an attorney for advice or go to SCORE.

STEP 5: Register with your state for unemployment tax purposes.

STEP 6: Apply for a federal Employer Identification Number with the I.R.S.

STEP 7: Register with other agencies in your state, if required.

STEP 8: Register for a business license and other necessary permits (if any).

STEP 9: Create a website (optional).

STEP 10: Create business cards.

STEP 11: Create a flyer.

STEP 12: Make sure to have pens, notepads, and a voice recorder.

STEP 13: Have prepared contracts printed out.

STEP 14: Purchase a weekly planner.

Now that you're all set up with legalities and supplies, let's get started!

Chapter Two

GETTING
NOTICED

B ecause I began an auction business first, I went to many
auctions, noting purchase prices of items and what the
items were called. You might want to attend an auction or
two just to see a mass of items, their names, and what they
sold for.

Or, if you're in a major city, go online and gather a list of
estate sales close to you. Attend as many and as often as you
can, and stay at each estate sale long enough to *feel* how it's
done and to *feel* the way it's handled. Personally, I like sales
that are organized. Messy estates tend to make me want to
flee instead of peruse.

I can't guarantee the personnel will be generous with your
questions if you state you're there to begin a new competitive
business. However, you might find someone like me who real-
izes there's plenty of room for everyone and will answer some
questions to help you begin. If no one will answer questions,
you can still jot down item prices, sketch what they look like,
and then look them up online to see what they're selling for.
Then get to work getting your business out there!

1. Place ads in the local paper stating what you do, such as, "We handle large or small estate sales, managing the tedious task of *what to do* with family members' items."

    Submit a press release with any newspaper in your area, as press releases are *free*. Just call to see if you should mail the press release or e-mail a press release to the person in charge of said operation. The only thing is you won't know if they will or won't place your release, but if they do, it certainly is a perfect way to get out in front of many potential clients and customers. It's not just the seniors who look at the online ads or physical papers, as they generally have family who may be looking for a way to dispose of their mother's and father's items as well. Of course, Facebook it, Twitter it, Google+ it, or use any online presence.

2. Send flyers or postcards to attorneys in your area noting what your service is, and always follow up with an introductory call so they know who you are. The Internet is a fabulous resource for learning which attorneys are probate lawyers. These are the attorneys you want. Or call your local banks' trust departments and/or probate offices at the local court building, stating you're beginning a new estate sales business. If they have an estate that needs to be sold, let them know you'd welcome a call to give your company's options to family members.

3. Contact local real estate offices, informing them of your new business. In my area, Tuesday mornings are when all agents attend a business meeting of new listings and information. During these meetings, they love to hear from new businesses that may help them clean out the contents of a property so they can sell the home seamlessly.

4. When calls begin coming in (and they will!), set up appointments. I generally set up sales on Tuesdays, Wednesdays, and Thursdays, which leaves Mondays and Fridays open for rest or to view new estates. You'll figure out what days off you need to incorporate into your schedule.

5. Check with your city's main newspaper, asking if they have a special day when companies advertise for estate sales. In St. Louis, it's usually Friday, just before the Saturday/Sunday sale under the area of "Estate Sales." Newspaper ads are generally costly, but if your client insists on a physical ad along with the online ad, limit it to five lines, including the link to your online ad. Even with a limit of five lines, it might cost your customer upward of $200. In my area, we just place it online and I pay the monthly fee, which is nominal.

   Your five lines might read like this: *EstateSales-Victoria, 7/13 10-3, 7/14 10-2, 1234 Jane St, St. Louis, 63129, quilts-tools-etc., Photos: victoriagray. net.* Line width may vary.

6. For the first year or so, place notices/flyers of an upcoming sale at such places as local Laundromats, grocery information boards, and drug stores. Businesses such as the St. Louis Bread Company allow flyers on their information board. These are *free!* People are always looking for furniture or various treasures to make their home individualized. This puts your name out there, so do it!

Note: You may come across a small estate, which will only be a one-day sale, but most are two-day sales. Be flexible. Within short order, you will know if you have a one- or two-day sale. Commissions will vary with these.

Chapter Three

APPOINTMENTS, QUESTIONS, AND COMMON SENSE

When a potential client calls, never run to all estates! First and foremost, ask questions making sure you're not driving to possibly view an estate filled with garage-sale items, thus wasting your and the caller's time. Ask, ask, ask! I can't say this enough. Within time, you'll be able to judge what they *really* mean, like whether or not their items really are great items as they state or if it is just hype to get you to share some of your knowledge for free.

Questions to ask the homeowner when they call for an estate sale consultation:

1. Where are you located? You certainly don't want to drive 50 miles or more away unless you live in a more remote or isolated area. I live in St.

Louis, Missouri, therefore all my sales are within a reasonable distance. Certainly, I've traveled much farther for a sale, but *only* when I knew without a doubt via e-mailed or texted photos that the items were truly special.

2. Can you tell me what you have in the estate? Is it all furniture or are there any knickknacks? They'll tell you about their furniture but generally won't know what style it is. Thus this question: *Is the dining room furniture dark or light wood?* They answer light. Then you say, "It sounds like it may have been purchased in the '40s or '50s." Generally, I hear this type of reply: *Oh yes, that's when my parents were married. They bought it around that time.* That tells me it's a blond set. Now get this, blond furniture is in vogue and the younger generations are into retro/contemporary furnishings. Just look at many new items on the market and you'll see remakes of the baby boomers' era or the '40s and '50s. Since blond is in vogue, if you add photos of such online and note it in your ad, you'll more than likely sell it easily.

3. Is it true vintage? In the '70s and '80s, furniture was still made of wood but not usually the walnut or mahogany from the past. I ask if they know when their relative purchased, say, the bedroom set. Many times, they'll reference a major event like a birthday gift or anniversary gift in the '70s or '80s, and it'll probably be merely stained pine or another popular wood from that period. However, wait until you view the estate to make any final notes on style. *Always* look up furniture

styles or carry a catalog filled with furniture styles and pricing of furniture from your local bookstore. As you do this, you'll soon note the styles and pricing without the aid of a book.

4. How many rooms are in the house? Is there a basement or a garage? This will help you determine the size of the sale.

5. Is the house packed with a lot of items or are there just a few? This will clue you into the setup time and whether or not you'll have many items to set up, price, and move.

6. Ask if any jewelry is to be sold. This is just for your information, as jewelry takes a great deal of time viewing, researching, and pricing.

After asking all the pertinent questions, ask the homeowner the best time to view the estate, giving them two dates and times to choose from. Jot the date and time in your weekly planner, calling the day before to verify the appointment.

Now that you have an appointment to view your first potential estate sale, follow these suggestions.

1. Always, always present a business card, stating your business name, number, and what you do. They need to know who you are and that you are who you say you are. Show your driver's license, if needed. With the craziness of the world nowadays, building confidence with your customers is a must!

2. Be conscious of your seller's feeling of safety. Many of our precious senior citizens are women

and live alone. If you have children, as I do, take one with you, preferably one who is not unruly. My four children grew up with the estate sales business and learned early on that they had to behave as this was Mom's business, and they always had to respect others' property. This was and is an excellent way for children to understand life and business. At any rate, children can break the ice when you first meet. If you're a man, please find a woman to join you at least when you make your initial appointments. Many seniors are wary of male callers. If you don't have a woman to bring with you, offer to first meet at a local coffeehouse or ask if they have a friend or family member they'd like to be present. Remember, safety first for all concerned!

3.   Look out for your own safety. *Never ever* go into an area that you already know is unsafe. Please take someone else with you and don't go at night. Questionable areas still have families who need to disperse of parents' items, but be safe at all costs. I have had to decline some area sales. It's not only the homeowner that must be cautious, but you as well.

Just a few months ago, a woman called me, frantic to sell the items left in her apartment because she recently married. I asked what items were left, and she gave me a list. From this list I thought a one day–only sale might suffice. However, I had to view the property to assess the best way to handle her sale. Since there wasn't much, according to her, I thought about it a bit further after we hung up. I then called an auctioneer I knew to see if perhaps he would just buy the contents. He said he'd be glad to look it over and get back to me, so I set up an appointment with the owner.

The seller was nonstop in wanting me to be there with the auctioneer, so I said I'd drive over, too. It just so happened I was viewing another sale several miles west. As I drove toward the location, I kept noting the neighborhood was becoming worse and worse. I turned my car around, and my phone rang. It was the auctioneer. He said, "Victoria, please don't go there. She has at least a dozen cats in there that have ravaged the furniture and it's not a safe area."

As I drove away, I called the seller and let her know I wasn't coming. She pleaded with me to go there anyway, but I knew better! She wasn't happy, but I was safe, and the auctioneer was, too.

4. If you do enter a seller's home, introduce yourself and whomever you brought along upon arrival. Give them your business card as you step in. Ask what they would like to sell. Many times, they have a list or have made mental notes, but you should have a tablet and pen or your phone recorder—whichever seems appropriate for you. I use a pen and paper; it's just easier for me. I used to draw a picture of a piece of furniture. However, with the advent of a digital camera, I now snap a shot of any and all items so I can check the price in a book from my collection, the bookstore, or online.

    Sometimes you may have a homeowner who can't move everything out before your sale.

Let them know that you'd be more than happy to move the items to one corner, cover items with a sheet, or place all items not to be sold in a separate room, closet, or porch. Don't let those items stop your sale. The customer will be happy you have a solution to something that had possibly been worrying them.

5. Walk through the entire house, asking if they mind if you open their closets and drawers. They want you to sell their items, but you must be informed as to what they have, so don't be bashful. You have to see the items if you are to do the job properly.

6. If you note that only the "smalls" are of interest to you, let the owners know. Perhaps the furniture is early toss-away that has been ravaged by dogs now removed from the home. This furniture needs to go to the dump so all that's left are the smalls. Smalls include cut glass, figurines, fine china, cups, saucers, and miscellaneous dishes. Various pots or vases such as McCoy, Weller, or Roseville are all fabulous finds! Some pots or vases may have signatures at or near the base; these will bring extra revenue, so *always* look closely at the items. I rarely tell a homeowner the value because, invariably, many homeowners will want to keep them and you want them as *pullers*, or items to pull potential buyers to your sale. If they only have smalls, you may want to do a one-day sale, adjusting commissions accordingly.

7. Get a signed contract, (see **pages 29–30**). Review the entire contract with the homeowner and discuss fees. Typical commissions are as follows:

    - Commission on cars: 4 percent
    - $0 to $5,000 commission is 30 percent with a minimum of $1,000, whichever is greater
    - $5,000 to $10,000 commission is 25 percent
    - $10,000 and above commission is 20 percent
    - Advertisement other than online is paid for by the consignee—from sale proceeds.

    There are generally no packing fees or personnel fees unless otherwise stated on the contract. The circumstances of each estate will determine if such is needed.

Chapter Four

REVIEWING THE CONTRACT WITH THE CLIENT

After you've viewed the entire estate, ask the client if they want you to handle their sale. If they say yes, bravo! You did a great selling job! And now it is time to sign a contract with them.

It's very important not to skip the contract process. Read the contract over with the client so that, without a doubt, they know what it says. They may have questions along the way, which means they're listening. Some will be very upset with the loss of their loved one and may veer off at times. Just be patient with them.

1. Find a comfortable place to sit, preferably with chairs and a table. Oftentimes the house will be upside down because relatives have rummaged through it.

2. Give the client a copy of the contract so they may follow along as you read the entire contract.

3. Have a date book or calendar for reference to agree upon the date of the sale. Then, of course, write in the information in the contract.

   It's important to ask the client if their name should be on the proceed check or if it should go to "the estate of Jane Doe." Oftentimes the person you're speaking with is the executor of the estate, which may be reflected in the contract, as well.

   I've had people contact me months in advance before they're actually ready for a sale, for whatever reason. Thus you may or may not get to this point, but I must add that if you've made them feel comfortable with you and your services, they will call you back when they're ready.

4. **We do not allow family members at the sale, as this can and has lost sales for clients.** Grieving people may be more attached than they think and might hinder the sale. In my early years, family members would step in front of me to stop a sale. My rule is no different than a real estate sales person showing a house without the owners there.

   Often customers at an estate sale have little compassion for those left behind. They may blurt out hurtful things like, "Look at this piece of junk; who'd ever want that?" or some such nonsense. I'm very used to these remarks, and because I'm not emotionally connected to the items, it matters not what someone may say. However, it would certainly hurt family members' feelings, causing them to want that potential buyer to leave.

5. Establish what items the client wants to keep or move out before the sale, or if they want a **reserve** or a set price for an item. I will only reserve pricing on five items, and no more than that, because sometimes clients believe their items are the best of the best. Sometimes they are, but that's the exception and not the status quo.

6. Tell the client that **first-day prices** are firm. I hold to that unless I have a customer who wants to buy a large portion of items on the first day. Of course, by this time, I've researched any and all items and know what should remain firm or what can be lumped into a reasonable group lot, which rarely happens on the first day.

7. Having a **second-day half-off** works beautifully to clear out the items. There have been times when the house is so packed that on the second day, I bring in plastic grocery bags and hand them out at the door when we start. Buyers can fill up the bag for $5 or $10, whichever seems appropriate. I also add that no lamps, small tables, paintings, or the like are to be sold in this format, but that those items, as with all other larger items, are half off. Customers just love this, and tons of merchandise moves easily this way.

8. Make sure to include the **address and dates of the estate sale** in the contract. Often, the client wants to know the date and time the sale begins and ends each day. I gladly write it in. Generally,

I start later than other estate sales, which allows more customers to come to my sales. Why? I learned early on that most estate sales in my area and surrounding areas start at 7 or 8 A.M. on Saturday or Sunday. This meant that if I started mine at the same time, the same customers would be at other sales instead of mine or vice versa. I usually begin my sales at 10 A.M. on Saturday and run the sale until 3 or 4 P.M. On Sundays, I begin at 10 A.M. and end at 2 or 3 P.M. Starting later meant my crew and I didn't have to get up so early, but the run time depends on the amount of items in each sale.

9. Unless the client pushes for a particular weekend, I acknowledge which weekend they want to denote for **postponement**, and I watch the extended weather forecast for 10 days out. I've only had one sale postponed to the following week because the estate was down a hill, and it was a very icy day. Online ads allow me to change the date easily.

10. It's important that the client knows ahead of time when you'll contact them with their **final figures** after the sale is completed. I'll ask if they want a text or a phone call of the total since most are into texting. But if they aren't, then I'll certainly make a courtesy call on Monday evening, also stating that the proceeds are sent via registered mail by the following Wednesday. I've reviewed other estate sale companies' terms and conditions online and saw that one estate sales company in my area takes two weeks before they send off the proceeds, which is just way too long to me!

I make sure that my client knows the reason, too. I try to take off Mondays and Fridays; however, very often I'm running to another potential estate sale. Thus it may be Monday evening before I settle down to tally up the figures. Clients usually understand. You don't want a client to worry about their proceeds at all. If they do, they won't give you a referral, and that's how I obtain most of my sales. This can't be stressed enough: *word of mouth is the best form of advertisement.* It's the bread your butter is spread on.

11. Your estate sale company's **right to withdraw** has to be in your contract. I only had one sale that I withdrew from, and it was 45 minutes before the sale was set to start. The female owner called me on a Monday, frantic to sell some of her treasures to make her house payment by that weekend. It was a referral, so I took my brother with me and drove to her home early one evening. She was kind but seemed a bit anxious, understandably so.

Even while we were there, she took a phone call, chatted, and came back to us to say, "I'm trying to get a job, but that man said first I had to get my head on straight." My brother and I looked at each other thinking the same thing. Should we or shouldn't we take this sale? I always feel for people in distress, so I took the sale.

I only had a few days to set up, take pictures, upload them online, and handle the sale. The seller didn't let me begin until the Thursday morning before the sale! With her help and no crew, we moved things around in her split-foyer home. All the while, she kept *trying* to tell me how we should do it.

I stuck to my guns, and it looked great when I walked out Thursday evening. But when I returned Friday morning, she had moved things her way. I was livid! Fortunately, she paid for the ad, with a check up-front Thursday morning, which I promptly cashed before I began the setup. I had no money out of pocket, just my time.

Again, when Friday evening came all was priced and set for a terrific sale.

When my brother, Dwayne, and my daughter, Ashley, met me at the sale, the client had again moved everything in the basement into the walkways, which meant nobody could view the items. I told the client there was no way I was handling a sale there.

I took down the checkout table that I had placed in the living room Friday. The seller grabbed my arms and squeezed, saying, "You have to do the sale! I have to have money!" I did not yell but firmly told her I wouldn't do more work for her after she had changed everything I had set up. My brother stood close by. She kept hold. I knew how to pull my arms downward to release her grip, something my tae kwon do black belt son Caleb taught all of us to do when someone grabs you like that. My brother quickly stepped in and supported me.

My family and I were out and in our cars within minutes. The client stood there astonished that we wouldn't do her sale. I said, "I'll leave some of my signs. Customers will still come because it's advertised online and in the newspaper. You'll be okay." I'd placed 10 signs out along her curvy roadway.

12. On the contract, I include language for **trash removal**. You'll have to find someone to do your cleanouts, or perhaps your crew might do that as well. However, I might caution you with the latter. Clients might think you didn't sell all their items and held them back for removal with the cleanout. There are plenty of people that need work on Craigslist, so try a few out.

Sometimes my usual $350 minimum is too high and or too low. Cleanout people have to factor in expenses such as their helpers, the fee to dump trash, and gas. They are not just picking up furniture but all the items left after the sale, including trash. You'll have to adjust the amount according to each sale and the remainder that's left. It takes a bit of try-and-see what works best, but you'll soon catch on.

13. The **commission schedule** I provided in the example can be utilized, or you can figure out your own commission schedule based on your local going rate.

Generally, in my area, 30 percent is utilized based on what's there. In my contract, I state a flat fee of $1,000 or 30 percent, whichever is greater up to $5,000. If the customer has been referred to you and there's little in the estate, you might want to change the percentage to 35 percent and only handle a one-day sale, thus having to pay employees for fewer days worked and still enabling a referred sale. Always view the estate to know approximately how many workers you'll need and how much time you'll need for set up and formatting photos. *Don't ever quote a fee over the phone without first viewing the intended sale, no matter how pushy a potential client may be.*

Since you've already viewed the contents, you should have a good idea of how much you think the contents will bring. This will enable you to state your fees based on what *you think* your return will bring. But I caution you not to divulge this figure to your sellers because that's what they will then expect, and you can't pinpoint who will show up at the sale and how deep their pockets will be.

I make sure to ask what, if any, items the client or their family members will be taking. Sometimes they take most of the finer pieces, which in turn means I have to charge a larger percentage, such as 35 percent, to cover expenses and income for myself and workers. I won't take a sale if the remaining items are garage sale items. Even if the family takes most of the finer pieces, they generally won't take all the finer pieces, and there will be enough for a decent sale.

14. Include the **advertising fee** *if* there is to be one. Look in the newspaper, find an estate sale, and call the local paper to ask what an ad that size costs. Generally, in my area, a classified ad runs anywhere from $18 to $20 per line or more. A small ad will run around $175, but I always write in $250, thus covering any extras I see that should be placed within the ad. Also, there are several *free* online photo albums available. I utilize a photo site/cloud to upload all photos

taken at the estate sale. Then I add the link to my website. Customers view photos via the link, which in turn costs the client less for their print ad. Not only does it enable customers to view the items online, but it also helps me know what I may have to research before the estate sale. *You will definitely want to purchase a digital camera for this purpose. I know many use their cell phones; however, the quality just isn't as good.* I also work in a program called Photoshop, which is all I need at present.

15. Make sure to have an **address other than the house you're working at**. Why? Because no one probably lives in the estate any longer. Obtain that *other* address and phone number, so you know where to send the proceeds.

16. **Sign the contract.** Make sure the client signs it, too.

17. Give the customer a **copy** of the contract and keep one for yourself. I now take along a portable scanning device for my copy and give the client the original. Giving them the original doesn't change anything except it saves paper and ink.

ADDITIONAL THINGS TO KNOW

If a physical paper ad is requested, the customer may ask if they have to pay for the advertisement up front. Since I have an account with the local newspaper, I just charge it to their final costs and pay the bill off the top of the sale, which is stated in the contract. I also print out a copy of the ad with their final paperwork.

Once the contract is signed and to help the client see what I can do for them, I walk around the house, picking up a few items and telling them what this or that might bring at their sale. **NOTE:** *I limit this to only a few items that I'm really sure will sell at the quoted amount, or perhaps better. I'm not giving them an appraisal, just a general idea.* They'll be astonished that a tiny little piece of Limoges is actually worth $50 or more, and they'll be equally interested in what they should throw away prior to the sale. Many times I have to tell clients a host of items that should be trashed and what should be left for sale, but only after they sign the contract.

If the seller hasn't removed the wanted items yet, I implore them to take everything out at least a week before I come to set up the sale. This makes it 10 times easier to prep a sale since I don't have to move their items around or locate a corner to stash them in, out of buyers' sight.

At times, the house hasn't been sold yet, and the client will stay there even though we're to sell all items noted. At these times, I just tell them to have their family members, if they have any living close by, take one bedroom and place all items they are to keep in there. Then we'll place orange tape across the closed door, marking the room as NFS (not for sale). Generally, everyone respects this.

THE MESSAGE I WANT TO COMMUNICATE TO YOU IS:

1. *Each sale is different.*

     Antique furniture 20 years ago was the trend and sold like hotcakes. However, people in the Baby Boomer age bracket have pretty much bought what they liked. And now the next generation wants a fresher look. Guess what's in vogue now? Nope, not Victorian-style antiques, but retro furniture! Anything from the 1940s, '50s, '60s, and '70s is selling, even if it needs repairing. There is still an array of beautiful Victorian and later pieces that sell for enormous amounts at high-end auction houses. So don't rule out that sector just yet. You just might find a very valuable piece in someone's home, and if you do, you need to advertise, advertise, and advertise it to pull in top collectors.

2. *Each commission is different.*

    Commissions are different based on content. Either there's enough for a sale or merely junk that would do best in a garage sale, which means you politely thank them for allowing you to view their estate and say a quick adieu. Don't waste any more time once you've decided it's not worthy of a sale, and move on to the next appointment. I won't even view an estate if all the questions I asked over the phone enlighten me as to the estate's garage-sale items.

3. *Each customer is different.*

    There's no doubt about this one. I've met various types of people in this business, which is something you can't really prepare for, although you can prepare to be diplomatic at all costs. Even if you don't hit it off with one family, you can count on being a smash hit with yet another. Some potential customers call you for advice never intending to hire you. When I notice a caller only wanting prices for their items, I politely stop the conversation and state, "If it's an appraisal you want, I charge extra for that. Is

that why you called me, or do you actually want
an estate sale?" I don't pull any punches, but
I'm never mean. I just don't want to waste my
time nor theirs. Out of respect, they shouldn't
have called with other intentions, as I get paid for
appraisals, too.

Then again, you'll meet the nicest people
along the way, and generally most are very
cordial. Some clients just get it and realize they
don't know anything about this venture and
allow your advice and judgment to handle the
sale in a business-like manner.

On the next page is a contract you may wish to utilize
until you can customize it for your own needs. I usually have
to tweak this yearly, and **I still read the entire contract with
each customer before they sign on the dotted line.**

ESTATE SALE CONTRACT

Agreement made this ____day of_____20_____ between_____

And____Victoria Gray_____ hereafter called Estate Sales Personnel.

The Estate Sales Personnel hereby agrees to use her professional skill, knowledge, and experience to the best advantage of both parties in preparing for and conducting the sale.

NOTE: We do not allow family members at the sale as this can and has lost sales for clients.

The seller hereby agrees to turn over and deliver to the **Estate Sales** persons, to be sold at a public Estate Sale the items at said address. No item shall be sold or withdrawn from the sale prior to the Estate Sale except by mutual agreement between seller and Estate Sales Personnel. <u>If an item or items is/are sold or withdrawn Estate Sales Personnel shall receive full commission on the item(s). And IF items are priced and sold, then appraisal fees apply.</u> Items to be protected at estate sale or taken from sale prior to sale are:

_____

_____

_____

The Estate Sale is to be held at: _____

_____

Sale weekend date: _____

And in case of postponement because of inclement weather, said Estate Sale will take place on a later date agreeable to both parties.

The Estate Sales Personnel <u>**will send a cashier's check and or money order with net proceeds**</u> **from sale within three days after sale, along with sale records. (This allows all customer checks to clear the bank.)** The seller agrees that all expenses incurred for the advertisement, promotion, conducting said sale, **and/or cleanout fee** shall be first deducted from the proceeds realized from said Estate sale before the payment and satisfaction of any liens or encumbrances. **The Estate Sale Company reserves the right to withdraw from sale IF homeowner and/or family members become hostile OR homeowner refuses to comply with contract OR safety is an issue. <u>All time and expenses incurred are due and payable should this transpire.</u>**

> Approval initials are required for cleanout crew to remove **unsold items and/or trash removal (same day, weather permitting)** after sale's end.

Seller agrees to pay all sale expenses including:

Estate fees_____

Packing fees_____

Other Personnel_____

Advertising_____

Other, e.g., Cleanout fee_____

X_____   X_____

   Estate Sales personnel signature   Seller's signature

                                     _____

                                           Telephone

                                       _____

                                       _____

                              Seller's address, city, state zip

Commission Schedule

- Commission on cars is 4%

- $0 to $5,000 commission is 30% with a minimum of $1,000, whichever is greater

- $5,000 to $10,000 commission is 25%

- $10,000 and above commission is 20%

- Advertisement other than online is paid for by the consignee—from sale proceeds.

There are generally no packing fees or other personnel fees unless otherwise stated on the contract. Circumstances of each estate will determine if such is needed.

Chapter Five

THINGS YOU'LL NEED TO SET UP AND HANDLE A SALE

Here is a list of some of the items you'll want to acquire to set up your estate sale.

1. Business cards—for potential customers and future sales

2. A website—You can google free blog sites: there's a ton out there! Free sites are just as good as paid-for websites. Then buy your domain name using an online hosting site and forward it to your blog.

3. Signage[1]—purchase at least 6 to 8 signs, 18-by-24 inches, and sign posts. These two-sided signs need to have arrows pointing in the same

direction on each side, for customers to follow whichever way they drive onto your sale street. By all means, purchase the heavier posts as the thin cheaper ones will cave in with the first frozen ground, which is a costly mistake.

4. Folding tables—I use resin tables that fold up, have handles, and that are easy to move and carry.

5. Cash box—standard metal box with key lock. Have $120 to begin your sale with two $20s, four $10s, four $5s, twenty $1s, and at least five dollars in quarters.

6. Up-to-date cell phone with a credit card device— to take credit cards

7. Numbered business-size cards for early customers who want to be first in line for specialty items and who arrive long before the sale begins on the first day. Store-bought cards can work, but customers often throw them away or tear them up. I find it less costly to make my own as needed.

8. S-hooks—for low-hanging light fixtures

9. Over-the-door hooks—for specialty clothing

10. Stickers—various colors

11. Safety pins—to tag doilies or other items

12. Large tags—for specialty clothing

13. Small tags—for jewelry and watches

14. Display case for jewelry and/or smalls[2]—a rectangular tabletop box with glass top that can be lifted for closer view and customer purchase

15. Calculator with both batteries and cord—since some electric outlets don't work in older homes

16. Beer flats or soda flats—these are the rectangular cardboard 2-inch-tall flats at the base of beer, soda, or canned goods from any grocery store. For silverware and miscellaneous smalls.

17. Masking tape—this does not harm walls or paint

18. Black felt-tip pens—for pricing

19. Ink pens

20. Notepad—for people to leave their phone numbers or e-mails for the next sale

21. Grocery bags—either plastic or paper

22. Various sized white labels—to label zippered baggies for jewelry or other smalls

23. Newspaper or tissue paper—to wrap fine pieces

24. Computer-generated signs, if possible, in plastic sleeves—for reuse. For example:
    Estate sales company is not responsible for accident or injury. (A homeowner's policy covers this or you can obtain your own insurance.)
    All children must be accompanied by an adult.

All items as is.

All sales final.

No refunds.

No smoking on the premises or inside. (This eliminates damage and picking up unsightly cigarette butts after your sale.)

Watch your step. (With arrows.)

More in Garage.

More in Shed.

WHO TO HIRE?

While he was in the navy, my father was in charge of 30 men on Merchant Marine ships as their armed guards. He had to be firm with his men. He found that if he praised them for something positive they did, they'd try harder to rectify something that paled in comparison. I try to do this as well, but at times, it just goes in one ear and out the other.

Most of my workers are semiretired or retired. Periodically, younger ones, eager to learn the business, work for me until they feel confident to go it alone. Often they start as buyers, selling their items at antique booths, thinking my job is simple, which it is for me. However, it's taken a great deal of tenacity and staying power to learn all there is to run a smooth estate sale. You can certainly do this business if you have persistence and love to learn!

I've gone through quite a few people over the years before finding which ones actually listen to my instructions of how a sale is to be handled. Even so, I still acquire some workers who, without knowing what my client and I agreed to, will blurt out something to the contrary. I quickly take the employee aside and kindly but firmly correct them. If they continue, I let them go.

You'll find people that will ask to work for you. If so, try them out. They might be keepers!

Since I'm only getting younger, as are my workers, I clearly state that we no longer lift or move large, heavy items and that *if* you buy something heavy, you *must* have someone to help lift and move it. I have to take care of my workers at all costs, as they are extremely valuable to me!

Chapter Six

SETTING UP THE SALE—LIFE AFTER LIFE NUANCES

To me, setting up the sale is the best part of the job because I get to rummage through a person's estate and it's all legal! Even though it may be fun, in the beginning of my career, I would become bothered by the fact that the home needed a sale because someone had passed. However, after the first year of feeling sick in the pit of my stomach regarding their loss, I realized that I was, in fact, aiding the customer with a task they preferred not to delve into. Without my help, they wouldn't have any idea what is saleable or trash.

Off and on throughout my career, I've seen and/or felt an interesting presence at various estates. I've always thought that I've had a connection to a higher power, and this business has done nothing but solidify that feeling. You may come across this if you're a sensitive person, too.

One such time was soon after arriving at a house just outside the hub of St. Louis city. I had instructed some of my crew to work in the basement and another woman to work with me in the shotgun side of a two-bedroom home. This estate was packed to the gills! This meant we had to stay focused in one area, pulling out all the items within a room, but this one had so much that it took extra days to finish.

After several hours, we pulled out and set up everything in the living room where the main entrance was. Subsequently, we moved to the adjoining dining room. We took all the items from the very full china cabinet, buffet, side shelves, and table tops to neatly set them up on the dining room table and a table I had carried in. As we were doing this, I felt a presence, looked over my right shoulder, and turned around to see a dark whoosh at the entry door! I saw a male figure wearing a red-and-black plaid shirt that quickly darted into the home and vanished just as quickly!

I turned to my co-worker and exclaimed what I saw. She calmly said, "Again?"

"Yes, again!"

She went on about her work, not fazed by my vision, because it's happened quite a few times over the 10 years she had worked for me.

I sensed in my heart the reason he showed himself was because he was worried about his wife. The lawyer handling the estate later informed me the original homeowner had left this life the year before and that the wife was doing okay in a retirement/assisted living establishment.

We only handled the three rooms that first day, on the right side of this house, which included the living room, dining room, and a back room. In these three rooms, I noted several family photos of a man and woman in business attire perched on the shelves and walls. No plaid shirts were visible in any photo. But I knew this spiritual being was certainly the late husband. When I went home that evening, I knew I had to talk to this spiritual being the following day and devised what I'd say to him.

The next day, my crew and I entered the house once more to continue the setup. I directed the workers to various rooms and went back into the living room for the one-sided chat I had prepared for the night before. I stood at the entrance where I had last seen him and noted a slight coolness in the air. Was he there? I believed and felt it to be so.

"Sir, I saw you here yesterday and I felt you're worried about your wife. I've handled numerous sales over the years and will make sure your contents bring as much as possible to help your wife. I learned she is in a retirement/assisted living home and is well taken care of. I know she misses you as much as you miss her and I feel you'll be reunited soon." After I made that statement, the temperature rose and I felt he almost nodded a *thank you* as his energy left.

What happened next clinched the deal that it was, in fact, the husband. I sent one of my workers to the kitchen to work, and I entered the front bedroom. Here I began pulling many beautiful quilts from the trunk to set them up on the now cleaned-off mattress as a staging point. When I went to the closet, I opened the door to find a closet full of plaid shirts! There were 30 or 40 plaid shirts in that small closet. I searched for one like I had seen on the spirit and found a few red-and-black plaid shirts, and one was actually made of flannel!

Then I knew for a fact this spiritual being was the husband.

On the **first day** of a sale, which my workers and I refer to as *pull-everything-out-of-everywhere day*, I start by figuring out where I want the checkout table. I choose a vantage point in the front room that allows me to see the entrance, which is the only door we keep open, and any adjoining hallways.

Second, my crew and I move furniture around to accommodate the table.

Third, I place a crew member in the kitchen to pull out all the items from the cabinets, top to bottom, often utilizing the cardboard flats to house silverware and or smalls. The cardboard flats are also a great way to display sets of glasses, which allow a customer to pay and carry out their purchase easily.

Fourth, the men generally work in the garage and or basement, whichever has more items. I usually handle the living room, dining room, and bedrooms. I make a point to move any furniture that has sharp corners to keep customers from harm's way. For each bedroom that has a bed, I pull off all bedding, folding everything neatly on top, creating staging points. If extra tables are needed, we carry several in from my car, strategically placing them for optimal viewing of merchandise.

As the day progresses, more and more items are set out on tables, floors, beds, and counters. Then I pull all items that warrant better exposure due to a higher purchase price. Most end up on the tables in the front room, where I watch them during the sale. Also, my workers bring items to me throughout each day, asking if this or that needs to be on the main table or not. By the end of the first day, my table is surrounded and mounded with items I need to sift through on the second day, placing them in a pronounced position for the buyers.

The **second day** consists of tightening up or better organizing the items we pulled out the day before. Once all is tightened, we begin using masking tape to tag all the items. I price all high-end items while my crew prices the everyday items, often asking if a price is correct or not. I walk the entire house to pull collectible items my crew may not have noticed.

All collectible items sit on my table or on the featured tables next to me. All extremely small collectibles get placed into display cases. I review all jewelry personally and check the back of each piece to see if there's an embossed jeweler's name. If there is, I research it online or in jewelry books until I know without a doubt its price. If I find it's of greater value, I price it separately utilizing a jewelry tag. If the jewelry is newer and there's no real gold, I bag it into baggies, placing a pricing dot or a piece of masking tape marked with the price inside and stapling it shut. Even though it's in a miscellaneous baggie, I still place all bags on my table.

During the course of the day, take pictures of as many items as you can. Be sure to turn items upside down or view the back side, taking pictures of all manufacturers' names to help you research the items.

During the evening, upload all pictures to your computer, adding all pertinent information to the estate sale websites, including dates and what's in the estate.

Anytime I am pricing jewelry, I check if the brand is one of the below, well-known brands. These brands draw crowds and higher prices:

- **Weiss**[1]—Weiss jewelry is always stunning! Created in 1942 by Albert Weiss, this line includes necklaces, bracelets, earrings, and pins. Quality is synonymous with the Weiss name.

- **Eisenberg**—The Eisenberg Company began marketing their jewelry during the '30s. It, too, is known for high-quality craftsmanship.

- **Hobe**—Pronounced *ho-bee*, Hobe has been a name synonymous with fine-quality costume jewelry since the 1920s. During Hollywood's golden age, Hobe jewelry was a favorite of Hollywood stars, and their finest pieces could be seen adorning starlets' wardrobes in many classic movies.

- **Coro**—The name Coro actually comes from an abbreviation of the original founders' last names, which were Cohn and Rosenberger. Coro's finest pieces could certainly compare in craftsmanship, design, and quality to well-known, highly collectible names like Weiss and Eisenberg. Coro also produced jewelry under other brand names such as Vendôme, which is highly collectible, Corocraft, Cellini, and Francois. Highly collectible Coro pieces include their famous "jelly belly" pieces, sterling silver pieces, including those marked MEXICO, and their "Coro Duette" line.

More collectible names include:

- Art
- Bogoff (Asaff[2])
- Boucher
- Carnegie
- Florenza
- Kramer
- Lisner
- Miriam Haskell
- Napier
- Sarah Coventry
- Schreiner
- Trifari
- Van Dell
- Whiting & Davis

In the bedrooms, when pricing clothing, I utilize individual tags for such items as luxury suits, dresses, skirts, shoes, furs, coats, and purses. If regular, day-to-day clothes remain in the closets, I create signs to hang next to the closets that declare the pricing.

Throughout each estate, I take photos of all the items and upload them to the already placed online estate sale ad websites, making sure all information correlates with the photos. If there's a ton of tools or other specialty items, they play center stage with star billing online.

For an average three-bedroom estate, my crew and I finish it within two days. Fuller or hoarder estates can take two to six weeks. When I have extremely full estates, I may have two or more sales, generally setting up the first floor within one or two weeks and handling the first sale that first weekend. The following week we begin on the second floor or basement, pulling items up or down to the first floor. Then, after setup of all those items, we have another sale. These two sales help clear the floors of items on both floors while allowing more room for display. If items remain after the first sale, the second sale will include them. I love these types of sales because that's where the big bucks are!

Another thing I love about estate sales is the fact that I see, hear, and feel the presence of ones that have passed. One such time was during a first day of setup. While in the second-floor bedroom, I kept feeling the presence of someone watching me. Each time I turned around to check that my workers were still on the first floor where I had placed them, they were where they were supposed to be. I continued to work even though I felt something strange around me. I could feel a woman's presence but was somewhat uncertain.

Just after the second-day setup, I took the usual pictures of the items around the home. When I arrived home to format and upload to the websites, I noticed one picture of an office desk along a basement wall that had over 30 orbs! The picture was taken when we had first arrived that morning before anything was disturbed. I knew I had to call the homeowner to ask a few questions and tell her what I saw and felt.

She and I chatted a great deal the first day I had met her, which was the same day she signed the contract. I had mentioned I often feel things at these estates, at which time she asked me to tell her about anything I might see or feel while at her deceased parents' home.

Thus I called her and told her about feeling a woman watching me on the second floor. She promptly said, "That's my mom. She worked really hard to have this house and her furnishings. I'm positive it's her making sure you took care of all her belongings." That made sense because the feeling I had was one of watching, which could mean she was seeing if I was tossing her items about or treating them with respect, like I always do. I didn't feel any sadness, just a watching. She wasn't there the second day.

Of course I followed with the story of the orb picture in the basement. Calmly, the seller said, "That was where my father's office was. He had an insurance company making use of the basement area every evening. I'm sure it was my father. He's been gone almost twenty years. I guess he wanted to make sure things went okay for my mother."

When I inform clients of what I see or feel, warmth generally encompasses them and a smile passes over their faces. It's very satisfying.

The pictures I take of all salable items and of the disorganized items before the setup often tell me many things. Here's something that recently occurred within my pictures, causing me to write this blog post:

Are they orbs or merely reflective circles?

I entered a plain two-story red-brick building dubbed a church by its pastor of 40 years and felt the calm that ensued inside. While he showed me each floor, including the basement, I knew that many stories were held within these walls. Especially upon viewing the small six-by-eight-foot cement baptismal pool that stepped perhaps four feet underground, painted a sea blue. I envisioned parishioners walking down the few steps into the pool of water, nervous, perhaps, but happy that they decided it was time for their baptism representing their closeness to their God.

Here I'd been invited to handle an estate sale of the pews, clergy chairs, bibles, baby grand piano, drums, mics, etc. As I walked about the first floor, I envisioned the choir that rocked the walls with their spiritual songs, clapping and stomping their feet with vast smiles abounding.

This photo shows orbs where these hallowed walls once rocked with songs of praise.

After viewing my photos, I decided to ask the pastor if some in the choir had since passed. *Oh, yes, we've had many come and go.* I didn't ask names since I wasn't there for an interview. I just nodded in sync with my thoughts and feelings. I wanted to know what others thought about orbs and did a bit of research.

Thus I've added information from two of the many sites that interested me. One online source states many claim an orb in a photo is merely a flash from a near-camera reflection.

Another source states, "**White or Silver Orbs:** Some investigators believe orbs that are either white or silver in appearance are an indication that a spirit is trapped on this plane. White energy is typically perceived as highly positive in nature."[3]

"**Blue Orbs:** Blue is spiritually associated with psychic energy and truth. It is a very calming color, and many people associate it with spiritual guidance. Some people feel blue orbs are a sign of a calming presence or energy, while others feel they indicate the presence of a spirit guide in that location."[4]

I looked up these colors because my pictures have white and blue orbs. I, for one, have come to believe that there is some sort of spiritual energy when my camera picks up an orb. This first photo was taken without a flash midday. There were no shiny objects nearby for my camera to reflect off, especially with no flash used.

The next photo was taken just a few minutes after. There was no glare from the window, plus the wood items caused no reflection, either. Many white and blue orbs abounded in both of these photos.

It was November 2015 when my crew and I were on the second floor of this St. Louis city church. This church was started by a kind gentleman, now near 80, who 40 years prior had a dream to help others. Thus he began this church. In the late 1990s, for five years he opened the second floor to homeless men. He gathered 14 twin-size beds, of which 12 were always full. Here he housed, fed, and encouraged all to obtain jobs and attend meetings that could and would help some to full recovery.

When I saw these orbs, I asked him, too, if any whom he had sheltered had died during those years. Sadly, he said, "Yes, I couldn't help them all." I knew from these pictures that these orbs, to me, symbolized those who had passed and held a connection to this once-safe haven. I also felt that they watched over all that entered this special meeting place on the floor below where many church pews and bibles used to reside and a host of members had attended the services. I felt these spiritual beings might possibly wonder where they should go next since the church is now closed. I wanted to take time to tell them to go into the light or at least to release their connection to this place as it would be torn down next year. But in my haste to handle the estate sale, I failed to take time to help them move on.

So instead of feeling poorly about not helping them move on, I decided to take with me the feeling that all is well. To me, they are a spiritual light and carry with them the kindnesses that this kind gentleman bestowed upon them while there.

I love estate sales for many reasons, but the best of the best is when I see a presence and, in this case, the orbs in the photos that encouraged me to ask more questions of what took place in this humble church. I think and feel I have a duty to pay attention to my feelings and, in this case, the orbed photos. By so doing, I may help some move into the transition of letting go of the physical, gaining stories along the way. Just like I do via estate sales, for those left behind when a relative or friend passes from their physical existence.

I once handled a small bungalow estate sale near Arsenal and Kingshighway in midtown St. Louis. As soon as I entered, the young granddaughter stated the piano to the right of the entrance was for sale. I personally wanted another piano because the baby grand I previously had developed a large crack on the underbelly, which was too costly to repair and thus I sold it. At any rate, this piano, a gorgeous mahogany spinet with Queen Anne legs and carved edging, jumped out at me. Quite the showpiece! The young lady stated they wanted $300 for it when the sale took place. I snapped a photo to show my father later that day over lunch. When I showed him, I noted there were all kinds of orbs all over it. I wondered who had played it and who had loved it so much to show up in a photo I had taken. My father, knowing how much I'd love to have it, pulled out a 100-dollar bill, followed by a 50-dollar bill, asking if I would be able to cover the other half on my own. *Oh my goodness, yes!* What a splendid gift!

My brother, Dwayne, called me a few hours after I brought Dad and Mom back to their home, asking me to join him for dinner. Goodness, I had no idea what was to transpire. After telling him of Dad's gift, he said, "Now I know what to give you for Christmas!"

Silly me, I asked, "What?"

He said, "I'll pay the other 150!"

What a blessed day that was! I didn't have to pay for the piano at all except for the piano mover! Now I have a gorgeous piano filled with love from the previous owner (at least, that's the feeling I got from her orbs) and my loving father and brother.

A few days later, when we began the setup, I asked the young lady about the piano and who had played it. She stated it was, in fact, the grandmother who played it almost daily and loved it. I didn't mention anything about the orbs because sometimes I get the feeling people won't understand.

Then there are those that seem to swish into a picture. One spring, I handled a sale in north St. Louis, where the daughter was in charge of her mother's estate. While setting up, I snapped a couple of pictures of a wheelbarrow in the basement. When I arrived home, I noticed there was a swish right in front of it. The daughter wanted to know if I found anything in her parents' home; therefore, when we went back the following day to continue the setup, I showed her the picture. With sadness in her voice but a smile on her face, she stated, "Oh, that was my father's wheelbarrow. He loved working in the yard. I know it's him. It's wonderful that he's there in front of it!" She hugged me, thanking me for that little tidbit of her father's presence.

Then later that spring, I had another estate where we handled two sales at one condo. It was so full, we had to set up the first floor and price and sell it before we could even think of selling the basement or the second floor. When I took pictures of the contemporary '50s buffet in the basement, it was a bit dark in the room as I hadn't found all the lights. Within the darkness, on my digital camera, I saw a swish of light cross the photo. I actually snapped several, making sure I saw what I saw. It was definitely a white swoosh! Later, I told the son who hired me. He stated the buffet was something his mother loved and had placed many of her small treasures inside. He, too, was pleased I spoke to him of it.

Another interesting turn of events took place at another sale. After the sale, a female client in her early seventies asked if I'd touch the motorized scooter her husband sat in just the day before he died. He died the Friday before our sale began.

When I stood behind his chair, touching the top, I felt a vast nervousness and stated such to the wife. She said he was very nervous Thursday night after hearing he had severe blockage to his heart. I then bent down, touching the arms of the chair, which seemed calm. I felt he was okay with his death and told the wife what came to me.

She was glad and added, "Victoria, I'm not upset that he's gone. Does that make me a bad person?"

"No," I replied. "I've felt while working here that he wasn't very nice to you."

"Yes, that's right. He was an alcoholic and a gambler. He gambled a great deal of money on a trip with our kids. He promised not to gamble and lied to me when he couldn't be found. He was never nice to any of us."

"I understand why you'd feel bad about not feeling sad, but I, too, had a tyrant of a second husband, and I wasn't sad at all when he died. In fact, when my father, mother, and I left the hospital that evening in 1989, I literally saw angels on either side of me lift a very heavy, wet wool coat off my shoulders and fly away with it to my right. I even told Dad that just happened, with a sigh of relief from his tyranny. No, you needn't feel bad about not feeling sad. You were his angel these forty years; you've served your time. It's now time for you to become free."

"But how do I become free, Victoria?"

I told her to close her eyes while I ran my hands an inch or so away from her head and down her torso, telling her when I finished to shake her hands as if to shake off his energy to the ground from whence it came. She did so. I also told her to do this before she went to sleep each night until she no longer needed to. She said she would and hugged me.

Naturally, I knew the angst was in her mind and heart, thus I ran my hands again about an inch from her shoulders and across her heart stating, "This is where you have to heal. You have to heal your heart and never feel bad about not feeling sad."

Immediately, she looked up at me, saying, "Victoria, I felt the energy from your hands as you did that! Amazing, isn't it?"

While we can't see the energy at work, we can feel its mighty powers. I said, "Please release each night to enable your complete freedom."

Also at this sale, two women came to my desk. One said, "Do you know how many orbs are in your pictures?"

This, of course, spawned a 20-minute chat. They told me of a St. Louis city hospital where one of the sisters worked and that it had much spiritual energy in the hallways.

We promised to keep in touch.

The following week, I wrote a note to a son and daughter about *their mother who had passed months ago:*

I must say, I've seen your mother three times in the condo! Twice, I felt she was in a doorway watching me, and the third, I actually saw a dark-haired woman walk down the hallway. I don't have a dark-haired woman working for me. Did your mother have dark hair? I know her kids do!

Interesting, I feel she's there, just paying attention. Is that a trait of your mother's . . . to watch over things?

The sister wrote back:

Wow! Yes, she had dark hair. Keep us posted on additional sightings or if she speaks to you. Thank you so much!

The son wrote back, too:

I think my mom would be very interested in the whole estate sale process. Getting a kick out of who was buying what. She was a very kind people person, very interested in others.

My response to both:

I felt she was kind too. Thanks for sharing a bit about your precious mother.

On the cleanout day when I vacuumed the entire condo, I kept feeling she was there, to my right, just viewing the process of which I felt she was quite pleased.

PAY ATTENTION, LISTEN, AND HELP GUIDE IF AT ALL POSSIBLE

The estate sales business has provided two newly built homes for me and my kids, travel money, and money to help others. Of course, it's not a steady income because selling clients' estates often comes in droves, and then there are dry spells. But I've learned how to manage my finances and roll with it knowing the universal energies are never ever late!

Years ago, a friend gifted me an enlightening book by Florence Scovel Shinn, in which she encapsulated the timeliness of universal energies: "As one grows in a financial consciousness, he should demand that the enormous sums of money, which are his by divine right, reach him under grace, in perfect ways. . . .

"I have seen the law work in the most astonishing manner. For example: A student stated that it was necessary for her to have a hundred dollars for the following day. It was a debt of vital importance which had to be met. I 'spoke the word,' declaring, Spirit was 'never too late,' and that the supply was at hand.

"That evening she phoned me of a miracle. She said that the thought came to her to go to her safe-deposit box at the bank to examine some papers. She looked over the papers, and at the bottom of the box, was a new one hundred dollar bill. She was astounded, and said she knew she had never put it there, for she had gone through the papers many times."[5]

I constantly ask the powers that be to send estate sales my way as often as possible, and they have never ever failed to do so! One such time in December, I grabbed my estate-sale date book with the thought that I needed one more sale to round out the year. No sooner did that thought ring through my being, then the phone rang. It was an estate-sale inquiry referred to me by a local real-estate woman.

The owner asked me to view his estate within three days. When we met, he said if his real-estate agent referred me and used me, then so would he! He signed the contract after a mere 30 minutes of showing me his huge home on seven-and-a-half acres. I set up and handled the sale the second weekend of December. The owner was so pleased that I could handle it so quickly because they built another home in Colorado and moved on December 1. Not only that, I use a great cleanout crew who did the cleanout the very next day. The house went on the market, clean as new!

Within this sale, I took many pictures, noting quite a few orbs again. This photo has 20 orbs!

This room previously housed many cat-scratching condos that we set up in the garage to contain the odor. The only lights in this room were two small table lamps. There were no overhead lights in any of the rooms throughout the entire home. Thus, I know the orbs were, in fact, real and not created from a reflective light source.

I'm sure many of their pets died in this room. There are about 10 orbs in this photo, too.

Pet owners surely want to know about their pets when they pass on, and this tells me that the owners were kind and loving to them. Why else would so many pet orbs reside in this room?

The feeling I got while in this house, and especially this room, told me the pets felt a comfort zone here and decided to linger in the feeling.

I know this couple hadn't had any children yet, and I knew that they loved their pets.

Since I don't have any pets, I can only tell you what I feel might be taking place. So I researched information concerning what others state on the subject. Here's one site that seemed to be perfect, and the only one I visited because it summed it up rather well.

"There are ghost stories about various types of pet animals, especially cats, dogs, and horses being seen after their death. Animal ghosts seem to visit where they formerly lived, and may stay for a minimal period of time or longer. . . .

"Upon a pet's passing, one should be alert to signs of the animal being with them in spirit, such as familiar sounds associated with the pet, a visible presence, or even an imprint or indentation upon a bed where the animal formerly slept. . . . This is also a good time to take photographs, as anomalies such as wisps of spirit, orbs, shadows, and even apparitions of the animal might be captured in photo."[6]

Then there are the estate pictures I'd love to see orbs in, and yet haven't found any. The following photo is of my father's favorite leather massage chair. He sat in this very chair when he had his heart attack on August 3, 2012. He'd been in the hospital for almost two weeks and asked to come home with hospice care for his final days. His wish was greeted wholeheartedly among his remaining five children. Each of us took eight-hour slots to help our sweet father during his last days.

Thursday, August 16, just four days before he left this life, I leaned into him on the right side of his face to kiss him and said, "Dad, if you're holding on for the kids, we love you so very much, but we don't want you to hurt anymore. It's okay if you leave. I'll miss the heck out of you!"

I can hardly write this, but he smiled and pulled me to his cheek, quickly rubbing his whiskers against my face. With a soft raspy voice, he said, "Take that with you."

That was the very last thing he said to anyone because, within the hour, he slipped into a coma.

My dear, sweet, loving father stayed here until August 20, 2012. There are no orbs because I feel he's moved on to the other side where loving arms were waiting.

We will never know the exact location until we, too, meet our relatives on the other side. I can tell you that I've telepathically chatted with Dad many times since his passing, typing each and every question and answer from beyond. He just loves it there!

I didn't really think I'd find any orbs lingering around in our family homestead in Affton, Missouri, but I kind of wanted to see one. But I know from chatting with Dad that because he longed to see his mother and father, he'd move easily on.

He was the best father a girl could have ever asked for!

Chapter Seven

BEFORE AND AFTER SETUP PREPARATION

Not all clients are pleased with the outcome of their sales. These clients are the ones that thought their items were worth more than the going rate. No one who owns an estate-sales business will please everyone.

I'm just happy to say that 98 percent or so of my clients are so tickled that their relative's items are sold. They didn't know how to price or sell them. Nor did they know how to organize the big mess the family created while digging through the estate.

I've gone into homes where mounds of items were truly thrown this way and that.

Before Setup

After Setup

Often resulting in huge heaps in the middle of a room, families will seek that one item that's been lost for years. Or perhaps it's something they wanted before another family member arrived. Either way, I tell all clients that no matter how messy an estate is, my crew and I will organize it to perfection for an Estate Sale by Victoria. They're always amazed that I hold true to my statement.

For me, it's the easiest thing in the business to organize a once mounded home.

This reminds me of an estate I handled back in 1999. One of the townships contacted the probate commissioner to clean out the estate. Thus, we were called upon to do so.

This hoarder's estate was literally filled with treasures. However, upon entering the small two-bedroom home in a very nice community, we had to move waist-high trash from the doorway to enter. I could not believe all the magazines and papers!

We had to stand on top of the papers while walking about the house, ducking through the doorways. And it only got better! At the back of this modest home, we noted the toilet no longer worked. The resident, since deceased, used to potty in vegetable cans and left them on the back porch! I kid you not! Oddly, there were no bugs in the house.

I hired men to carry out all the crap. (No pun intended.) Probate paid the bill, and we sold the remaining items. The sale was small, but probate was eventually able to clean up the house and sell it in as-is condition.

Whew! I don't like these types of estates, and generally I won't take them. But I had great helpers that did the entire cleanup. That was in my need-to-take-any-and-all-sales years to feed my four growing children.

Here's a story from one of the first estates I handled.

THE ARENA¹ AND A ST. LOUIS AVENUE ESTATE

One hot summer day in 1991, I rode with my auctioneer in an old red beat-up pickup truck to a home also in the same condition. We'd won the highest bid to buy out the contents from probate court earlier that week. Now that we owned the contents, we had to clean out any and all items that were sellable, and many were. Since I knew in advance that the house had roaches, I opted to wear knee-high boots, a long-sleeve blouse, and jeans tucked into the boots, along with rubber gloves. Heaven forbid a baby roach would touch me! Thankfully, I escaped undefiled!

The small, white, bacon-grease-smelling, disheveled, shingled 1930s-style house clearly stated—no, almost screamed—a sadness that roamed about. I recall feeling and envisioning a story-like sadness, where perhaps the mother walked to and cleaned nearby office buildings or took in laundry, too tired to clean her home properly when finally home from a hard day's work. Her hair would have possibly been washed once per week, piled upon her head in a bun while wearing a white rag-like scarf, dirty from each week's work. The father, perhaps, walked too, working down the way at the carriage factory on the other side of the highway, just making it by, week after week. Late in life, I found out later, the mother gave birth to a baby girl, the only child they had. Sadly, the baby girl had a mental disability, but the parents were ever so loving and kind.

This daughter, when in her teens, begged her friends and her parents to chauffeur her to the local bus to the Arena (built in 1929, closed in 1994) when boxing stars and or country western singers came into town. I was told she'd lean up against the stage, holding the free pictures given to all as they entered the Arena. There she and others begged the stars for signatures. Apparently, she gathered quite a mound of signed pictures, which I kept. I also still have a signed post-card by Jack Dempsey in 1957 and a pair of advertising-size boxing gloves he signed.

The auctioneer had no problem digging in the mounds of smelly household items. One of the finds was a collection of cobalt blue small pitchers advertising Shirley Temple, the sweet child star, singer, and tap dancer that I and the masses fell in love with on the silver screen or TV.

As the auctioneer pulled items out, I'd wash them in the large white porcelain sink, making darn sure I never touched the sink with my body. No roaches bothered the sink, but many scurried away as we walked about and he searched. Each time I washed an item, I carried it to the truck to pack it for our future sale.

You might wonder why I'd take on such a horrific job. As a widow with four children, I had—and by golly, would do—whatever it took to take care of my babies, even if the estate was a falling-down, smelly old place filled with valu-able vintage items. I'd do it and did so proudly!

The items brought in a great deal of income while at the same time carrying on the cycle of life.

I always feel it's this cycle of life that infuses new energy to each item, thus bringing joy to those that purchase and admire it until it's time for the cycle to run its course again.

I never know what treasures and stories await me when I'm commissioned each estate sale.

Chapter Eight

SALE-DAY PREPARATION— LIFE AFTER LIFE NUANCES

G enerally, I arrive one hour before we begin each sale day, placing 18-by-24-inch signs on strategic street corners and in the estate-sale yard. It's important to place the house sign in the middle of the yard as parked cars block it if it's at the curb.

The crew tapes my pre-printed signage onto the walls using masking tape, which doesn't harm painted surfaces and removes easily when the sale is finished.

We even have yellow caution tape, purchased at the local hardware store, and tape it on various thresholds or oddly set steps, giving a visual to alert customers to watch where they're stepping, thus preventing accidents.

This yellow caution tape is also used over low pipes in old houses or low-hanging light fixtures that can't be pulled up with S-hooks.

If not previously raised, we make sure that any hanging light fixtures are securely raised out of heads' way as high as possible. If this S-hook raising isn't quite high enough because the fixture is more stationary, we apply the yellow caution tape, draping it down low enough to make a passerby notice and duck.

I supply matching black aprons for all workers to wear, which in turn allows customers to know who to ask for help. Each apron houses a roll of masking tape for marking something sold and a black Sharpie.

I host the checkout table and strategically place my workers where clear visibility spots are. Usually, besides myself, there are three to five workers for Saturday and three to four on Sunday.

My workers help all they can to sell the merchandise throughout both days. Often, just chatting with a customer about something they clearly admire will spawn a sale.

Saturday's pricing is firm unless a customer wishes to purchase large amounts of items. Then I step in to price and finalize the sale. I'm up and down out of my seat all day, both days, helping customers, and I will place my brother in my stead at the checkout table.

It's like a symphony of people, swaying this way and that to dodge the chest of drawers being moved carefully down the stairs from the second-floor bedroom. Or the living room sofa, up and out the front door with, "Excuse me, coming through! Watch the glass door! Watch your elbows, the fixture is sticking out! Please hold open the door." Thank-yous abound because all who enter or leave seem to have a kindness and understanding about them. Not all customers are so lovely, but 99 percent certainly are!

Just like Bob, an 88-year-young gentleman. What a sweetie! A few months back I wrote this blog post about Bob.

Greet Every Day with a Smile

Days ebb and flow so quickly that I forgot to blog of customer Bob and what he said on Saturday, April 16.

When he arrives at my sales, he makes a beeline to my checkout table, always with a smile. I saw him coming and said, *"Hi, Bob. Glad to see you!"* He's 88 years young, you see, and wears a smile that lasts the entire time he's at my sales.

He walked over and said, *"When I peruse the estate sales online, I make sure I stop by the sale where the lady always smiles!"*

"Really?" I asked. *"I'm the smiling lady?"*

"Yes, you always have a smile for all your customers. You know, when I was younger, I had lots of anger issues and went to a doctor for it. That doctor told me that if I'd only wake with a smile and greet all my adversities with that smile, then all my troubles wouldn't seem so large. A positive attitude and smile changes how I see things every day!"

I know I smile a lot because my father also stated something similar. I asked him several years back, *"How it is that you always seem to smile no matter what?"*

"Well, honey. I learned a long time ago that I could either wake each morning with a smile and deal with the day or I could decide to be a grump every day. I chose to smile and that's how I've lived my life ever since."

Bob agreed and thanked me for always smiling and being pleasant to all that enter and leave my sales.

What a grand thing to note. It made my day that I make his day when he enters my sales. Oh, sure, there are clients and customers that curl my toes, but I always handle things with a calmness of spirit. Why should I stoop to any other level? That would only burn my insides, and they'd just walk out the door. No, I chose to smile. Thanks, Bob.

I'm such a people person that I could chat for hours if the conversation is enlightening and intelligent! Bob also came to my sale in March 2016 with this information, which I promptly blogged the next day, as follows:

World War II—Memories and Orbs

Last weekend, I handled another wonderful estate sale. Approximately 300 customers attended each of the two sale days. The rooms filled with smiles, oohs, and aahs as persons picked up this or that to purchase. By 1 P.M., Bob, a kind gentleman who visits my sales often, sat in a chair across from my checkout table. His smile reminded me of my precious father, Victor, now gone. Mr. Bob exudes the same vim, vigor, and kindness my father had, which makes me feel my father's presence.

Soon Bob began telling me stories of his time in the navy during 1947–1948 in the Marshall Islands. I jotted notes as his stories unfolded. He spoke of Kwajalein, Bikini Atoll, Likiep, and other islands where nuclear weapon tests took place and how when an undercover officer visited them asking questions, one private spoke way too much and was escorted back to the United States. Bob sat silently, later learning the man who listened was there specifically to *learn* which men divulged info and which didn't. He mentioned, too, that many mornings his shoes were underwater when the tide was up. It was extremely interesting and caused me to reread part of *The Ankle Express*[1], a book I wrote about my father's equally interesting Navy life.

My father's Navy years from 1942–1944 as an armed guard aboard Merchant Marine carriers are shared in the book. His stories in the Solomon Islands, the European and Pacific Theaters', Australia, and other ports of call are amazing! One of which included the Blitz while in Hull, England.

Switching gears . . . It's amazing how life on the other side comes through.

When my father is with me, I see a gnat swirling around my face. I know Dad is there. (Others, I'm told, see ladybugs or butterflies, familiar signs specific to them, letting them know a family member is with them, too.) This day, I saw the gnat only while Bob spoke of the navy. The gnat walked on my left hand, leaving when Bob left. It made me mist up and wonder if others appreciated my father's stories, like I did, and Bob's stories, as much as I do. Bob was even amazed and thanked me for listening. It was my pleasure, without a doubt! I wonder, too, how many diligently listened to my father's stories, perhaps as he cut their hair at his barber shop. At any rate, his stories will never be forgotten, since I wrote his life history, covering 385 pages. He was so pleased one of his children took the time to interview him and completed the book before his last month on earth. I salute you, my precious father and Bob. Keep those stories coming!

Also, at this home . . . in a few pictures were many orbs! In a conversation with the widower, I told him of the photos with orbs. One photo was of the large oval dining-room table, which housed at least 20 orbs. It was of this picture that I asked him if his wife worked at, knowing she sewed. When this photo was taken, I had no lights on nor were the window curtains open. He paused, looking at the table, and somberly said, "We had so many wonderful family dinners there with the kids and grandkids." Later, he asked if I'd send him and his son the pictures via e-mail. Well, of course, I said yes and did so that evening. The orbs are very visible and abound in both photos.

When I toured the slew of pictures I took for the sale, I also saw orbs over the twin beds in the basement.

A place where family often stayed when visiting, I was told.

The son told his father he saw *things* often, too, at his own home and would enjoy the pictures, stating how interesting it was to know his late wife and mother of his children was there.

So pay attention and tell your stories. People really do want to hear or read them.

Who knows, maybe one of your pictures shows a relative's orbs.

I have such lovely customers! Here's another blog I wrote so as not to forget.

Kindness . . . pays its way!

Last weekend at an enormous tool/estate sale a kind lady named Betty came up to the checkout table loaded with goods to purchase.

Betty thanked me for my kind words within the estate sale notices. I asked her which words she liked. She said, "You always add 'take care' or 'be safe,' and no other estate sale company ever seems to care about their customers like you do!"

I pondered her words, stood up, walked around my table, and hugged her for the kindness of her compliment.

I do wish everyone a safe day or to be safe until we meet at the sale. It's just my way. I truly love my customers. If not for them, my sales would not enable my livelihood, nor would I know the kindnesses they gift me in return.

Some, as mentioned in a previous post, state, "You're the smiling estate sale lady," and I love it!

You see, kindness goes a long way, and yes, it pays its own way via smiles, hugs, and yes, even with compensation.

When a business owner develops that one special trait, the business will soar!

My father's barber business ran the same way. So many walked into his shop happy, even though it was standing room only, till he closed it at age 81. Often, he told me, "Honey, I have the best job ever! We laugh and cut up all day long and I get paid for haircuts and tips. I just love my business." Because of his wonderful thriving business, he and Mom took us on two-week road trips every year I can remember, from the late '50s till I married in 1972. Trips included the Smoky Mountains (at least a dozen times, which was where Dad and Mom honeymooned), the Wisconsin Dells, the Rocky Mountains, Yankee Stadium, the Royal Gorge, Niagara Falls (both the United States and Canada sides), and so many states in between. All from the tips he saved each year! I didn't know then, but it was as if we were rich!

After my second husband died, I took all four children on numerous trips as well, from estate sales and previously auctioned profits. These were fun times with my kids, and these trips helped me acknowledge what a grand gift my father had given us each year and the cost it entailed.

Last weekend, Betty, with her hands full of goodies, asked, "How much?" I told her $30, but she handed me $40.

I said, "Here's your change."

She promptly said, "Oh no, you get that as a tip. You deserve it! I just love you and how kind you are to everyone! No, that's yours!"

I was taken aback because tips are rarely given in this business—until last Sunday. Generally, it's a thank-you at the end of the sale by the homeowners or the real-estate person who referred me. Money is usually spent on goods.

I'm pleased that kindness pays its way!

Please show kindness to one and all.

After the last table and supplies are packed in my SUV, the cleanout crew waits patiently to enter the estate to clean out all the remaining items. Note, this is only factored in the sale if the client has signed off on the box relating to this transaction. I then pay the cleanout crew foreman from the proceeds, leave for a few hours, and return to make sure they're doing all that's expected. They always come through!

Once the sale is finished and the cleanout crew is finishing up, I take off, knowing my job and theirs are well done.

Mondays, I've allotted for time off; however, I may have new estates to view for future sales. All monies are tallied Monday evening from tickets I use for calculation purposes only. Commission is taken off the top as well as the cleanout crew check. Final proceeds, in the form of a cashier's check, are sent to the relative in charge no later than the following Wednesday, via a Priority envelope.

Then the estate sale process begins again the following week. I've built up quite a following of over 21,000 customers, which in turn allows for a great deal of referrals.

Chapter Nine

PRICE SUGGESTIONS FOR CLOTHING

I t's very easy to handle estate sales, even if you aren't seasoned. Here's a list to help you begin pricing clothing. Nothing should be priced like a garage sale, which many people are used to. When beginning an estate sales business, note how pricing should be structured. Just this one step creates a higher-end sale as opposed to garage sales.

I mentioned earlier that I like organized sales. No, I don't go crazy, but I do make sure every item that goes with a grouping is moved to that grouping. Or all clothing is hung up in several closets with the closet doors open for viewing and, of course, purchasing. Generally, I create a price sheet, placing it on the closet door or a neighboring wall in this manner:

- **Coats**—If everyday and in good shape, $5. However, if you have a very special hunting jacket or a vintage coat, please price it according to your findings for such. If you price items way too low, potential customers, of course, will seek out your sales when word-of-mouth informs them of your low pricing *but* it lowers the pricing across the board for one and all estate sales. Just one item can ruin pricing for the others, and you lose money for you and your client.

- **Blouses**—Generally, I price them at $1 to $3 based on condition. And if they are all in the same condition and are basic-wear, I price them at $1 each.

- **Ladies' slacks**—Based on condition, I price them between $3 and $5 unless, of course, they happen to be a very special brand and are in mint condition. Then a higher price is issued and placed on *that item only* with a brief description so there's no mistaking that it's a special piece for such and such amount.

- **Men's trousers**—If they're in great condition, price accordingly. However, if you overprice, they'll just sit there. I price most day-to-day trousers at $5 to $10. If the trousers are dress pants, price accordingly and add a *separate price ticket on each pair* so there's never any confusion.

- **Ladies' hats**—There are not as many hats as there once were; however, there are a number of vintage hats out there and many Red Hat Society hats. So use your judgment on each and every one. If many of the hats are vintage and basic, just price them between $5 and $15 each. If they are exceptional in style, color, and condition, then check online to learn what that particular type/style has sold for.

- **Men's hats**—Price pretty much the same as ladies' hats. However, you may come across a Stetson, which men really like. Place $30 on it or more! You can always lower the price if you have a buyer who's fumbling over a few dollars.

- **Men's and women's jeans**—If worn, just charge $1 to $3 dollars . . . unless you happen upon very costly jeans and you know they are very likely to bring a higher dollar amount. Then price accordingly.

- **Shoes**—These go for maybe a dollar per pair. Rarely are shoes worn on a daily basis priced higher than that. If, however, you come across a pair of super-duper fancy men's or ladies' shoes, and you know they're worth more, then place a special priced ticket on such. Note: Shoes are not the easiest to sell, especially if they're extremely worn. I've had to throw away some of the good-old-broken-in ones.

- **Miscellaneous items**—May or may not be priced before a sale. At my sales, I verbally price what I call tchotchke (choch-ka) or miscellaneous smalls when a customer brings the items up to the checkout table. It's so much easier and saves me a ton of time.

I must say, I love the circle of life and how an estate sale can change a family's life with recycled furniture, clothing, shoes, or utensils that they may never have had the money to purchase! There's a kind gentleman from Bosnia who buys a great deal of shoes to send them to his homeland. His relatives eagerly await his packages. He, too, smiles as he rummages through the used shoes finding many less worn for his family. Others come to purchase clothing for local families, too.

I hear stories and stories of those less fortunate who, if not for customers looking out for them, may not have a bed, sheets, blankets, or the like for quite some time. It truly is a blessing for the client's family and those that buy.

Here are a few sample signs, which you can remake with your figures:

LONG COATS	$10
SHORT COATS	$5
SUIT & SPORT JACKETS	$5
SHIRTS	$2
SHORTS	$2
PANTS	$3
SWEATERS	$5
SHOES	$2/PAIR
BOOTS	$5/PAIR
SLIPPERS	$1/PAIR
BELTS	$3
SCARVES [SHEER]	$1
SCARVES [WINTER]	$3

BOOKS

LG — HARDBOUND $4

SM — HARDBOUND $2

LG — PAPERBACK $1

SM — PAPERBACK   50¢

NO SMOKING INSIDE HOME PLEASE

Chapter Ten

RESEARCH, RESEARCH, RESEARCH DELIVERS THE BIG BUCKS!

When packing an estate for auctions, I learned to separate what I knew to be the better glassware, jewelry, pottery, clocks, books, and knickknacks, which are called *fine collectibles* in this industry, from the everyday item. Because of my research, I learned what items were fine collectibles and what weren't. This knowledge helps me tremendously with estate sales in that I still separate better items from mundane everyday items within each setup. All small collectibles are placed on tables surrounding the checkout table where I reside most, thus preventing theft.

After separating the collectibles to sell at a special auction, I'd rent out a local recreational center to sell the moderate items once per month, saving the finer collectibles for a more defined, higher-end auction. This, in turn, meant I had to set up a special sale, which I did every six months or so, and these special auctions meant I needed to advertise on a larger scale to bring in the big hitters. If, and only if, you choose to buy an estate and sell perhaps at another venue, then this process is one to follow. However, once I stopped handling auctions, I no longer purchased estates, which meant I now handled the sales on-site in each client's home for a specified commission.

One such auction was at a local banquet center. I bought the entire estate here in St. Louis for $5,000, which is what the owner wanted out of it. Most of the items were packed in boxes, so I took a risk at this price. However, I was able to see just enough in this very, very packed three-bedroom house to note that $5,000 would certainly cover what I could see. Little did I know I'd uncover a ton of Anheuser-Busch beer mugs or a beautiful ornate cash register, or fabulous vintage furniture nestled under boxes and boxes of beer mugs. There were so many things to separate for a finer sale, which is where the banquet center came in.

Note the actual flyer I created to dispense at previous sales, thus whetting everyone's appetite for this sale. This is important to do, if possible, even for estate sales.

Pro-Q Auctions By Victoria

Sunday Sept, 29th
&
Monday, Sept. 30th

Estate of R....... D.......
Location: Banquet Center
1111 S. Lindbergh
Directions: From 270 (S) to Gravois (E) to
Lindbergh (S) to 1111 S. Lindbergh

Sunday: 2:00 till 6:00 pm – selling a beautiful 9' x 6' ornate back bar, plus outstanding collections of beer steins, mugs, beer signs, electric & neon beer-related pictures, and Wild Turkey decanters, i.e., Austin Nichols Wild Turkey decanters, Warner Bros. small decanters, Wild Turkey decanters—#1-1979, #2-1980, #2-1983, #3-1981, #1-1986, #1-1983, #2-1986, #4-W.T. & Eagle, #6-1985, #7-1985, #8-W.T. & Owl, #10-1986, #5-1985, plus President Decanters, several A. Busch collectors' truck and van banks and numerous other memorabilia.

This collection varies from the '60s, '70s, '80s, & '90s.

Monday: 10:00 a.m. till finished. Sellling Theo-A-Koch's Company Chicago Barber Chair, Gold Ornate cash register, 5-cent one-arm bandit and any remaining beer items and miscellaneous furniture, toys, memorabilia, etc.

Terms: Cash or check with proper I.D. When paying by check & unknown to estate sales company, must have bank letter of credit.

YOU WON'T WANT TO MISS THIS SALE!

You *may* need newspaper ads, too. A sample ad (make it short, which is less costly) under the category of *Estate Sales or Auctions* (whichever I needed) would read like this: 4444 Somewhere St.—Sat. 4/5 & Sun. 4/6, 8 a.m.–3 p.m. Antiques, collectables, linens, misc. Victoria 314-601-1899. Victoriagray.net.

With online ads, you may or may not need a physical newspaper ad. But I always place my phone number in every piece of advertisement. You want everyone to call to ask any question they may think of.

My company name now is **Estate Sales by Victoria**. It's very important to add your company name to any advertisement. Buyers begin to look for your name to attend your future sales if they are satisfied customers. And with 21,000+ followers to date, mine is the kind of following you want.

I also place in the estate sales ad that there are **no previews**. *Previews* means many buyers/collectors want to come before the sale is open to the public, hoping to buy all the great items before the public even gets to view them, possibly the day before the sale. I don't allow this for estate sales because once they learn you do this, many collectors will not come to any of your future sales. So it's up to you. I want all to come to the public sale. It's also a psychological thing if a potential collector has to purchase alongside a neighbor who is just stopping by. The collector jumps quickly on an item and will pay the top dollar you placed on a piece before another is able to purchase it. I have a lot of fun watching people and how they react at my sales. So enjoy!

By placing your ad in this way, you hit a wide range of people. Many also want to see what type of job you do at your sales, just in case they want to use your company for their future estate sale. I've obtained many, many sales this way.

I placed a similar ad for this particular auction in a midwestern auction paper, bringing in numerous collectors.

Note: At an auction, it only takes two people to bid against each other to raise pricing. Thus the audience count need not be large, just filled with collectors, and this auction was filled with them.

I have to tell you, this was one of the most profitable auctions I ever handled! Just the items we sold at the two-day sale at the banquet center brought in $23,000! Of course, the advertisement costs and employee wages were taken out of that. Now, it got better. After this first round, my crew and I went back to the house to sell the first-floor items, then the basement items, then a final sellout of the remainder items, which we did in place, meaning on the premises. By the final sale at this small three-bedroom house, the front and backyards were still packed. Even so, we sold it all! This, as stated, was an *auction*, but estate sales can be very profitable as well. It just depends on what's there and the research you do ahead of time. This continued research allows me to know what's selling currently and at what prices and what's dropped out of favor.

That sale did almost $50,000 total! Sure, there's always a risk in purchasing anything when you can't see the whole estate, however this is where research, knowing, and believing there's so much more than meets the eye comes into play!

Plus, I can't stress this enough—**research, research, research**! Gain all the knowledge you can about any and all items. Search online, of course, but don't leave out glassware, collectibles, antiques, and retro-/contemporary-focused books at the library or bookstores.

The owner of the estate I mentioned had already sold the house, and all had to be out within three weeks, which we were able to do with utter thankfulness from the owner. It took a bit of scrambling, but how grand the scramble was.

I always add a note of thanks for allowing my company to do their sale, along with several of my business cards. When they tell their friends, they can then give out my cards. It's free advertisement, so utilize it!

* ✳ *

Another terrific estate sale I handled took place at a tall, narrow three-story house in the hub of St. Louis city. It was clearly the best hoarder's house I've been privy to sell via an estate sale to date! It was amazing the items that rested there waiting for eager buyers to rush through the doors!

After the client signed the contract, I began figuring out how to handle this huge, filled-to-the-max house. It was so packed that when my brother and I unlocked the front, oval Victorian door, he had to push it open bit by bit with his shoulder so that we could squeeze inside to the parlor and beyond.

The widower told us that his late wife and he used to live there for a few years until she filled it to the max and he couldn't stand it. He actually bought another home across the street for him to live in! She, however, stayed in this packed house until she died a few years later. Astonishing, indeed! But I see and hear these stories all the time. Sure, some are less ostentatious, but all are interesting to me.

I decided to set up the first floor the best we could to have one sale within two weeks. This allowed me and my crew to sell as many items as possible from the first floor. Then we carried down items from the second floor, handling a sale two weeks later for the first and second floor. After we finished the second sale, we were then able to get to the third floor, which was filled to capacity with vintage toys of all kinds, including a wide variety of Tonka trucks, which are still sought after. I learned three sons came from this marriage, which meant three times the toys, all of which were from the early and mid-fifties. Added to this, there were Roy Rogers play guns, holsters, and so many items to sell.

When the sale opened, I was on the third floor with a cashier on the first floor. Oh my, the collectors swarmed that floor! I was actually pressed up against the wall as the masses grabbed this and that. I felt so pleased that I had advertised this sale to the max, and the collectors and all others were so tickled to find what they call a *virgin sale*, meaning it had never been viewed by any of the public before the sale. Pretty cool!

Thus, the third sale, which was on the sixth weekend, brought in a great deal of money that we tallied out at over $20,000! Of course, I paid the workers out of that and the client got his portion. Was he pleased? You bet! He couldn't believe his late wife had gathered so many great items, much of which she had scoured from the Dumpsters in the alleys behind their home. She may have been a hoarder, but it certainly helped him and me out.

Not all sales equal these amounts, but it's icing on the cake when one is delivered to me on a silver platter like this one and the others mentioned. Most estate sales range from $3,000 to $6,000. During my early years, I had to learn how to price things and how to factor in the commission, which was 20 to 25 percent. Now I maintain at least $1,000 minimum up to $3,300 or 30 percent, whichever is greater. This assures I make something while paying my crew. I take smaller sales all the time because it keeps my crew and me working, and my name is out online on an ongoing basis.

I did auctions for 10 years until I had to let the auctioneer go. Sometimes these shifts turn out to be a wonderful positive experience in one's life, as it was for me! And I have to say, I was tiring of the auction business. Thus, I decided to only handle estate sales and still do through this day. I just love them!

Chapter Eleven

FABULOUS FINDS

Every home has the basic sofa, end tables, lamps, Lladro figurines, low-end fine art, Waterford vases or figurines, or Anheuser-Busch beer steins. Since I began, retro clothing has been in vogue, too. Once in a while, though, you'll come upon some extremely valuable items featured on this special site.[1]

- Knoll International furniture
- Oriental rugs
- Art deco figurines
- Art nouveau bookcases
- Native American olla urn/basket
- Apache woven willow and devil's claw basket

- Brass cocktail table
- Lily Pad II dining table
- Cocktail shaker by La Maison 1928
- Pair of wall lights by Hans-Agne Jakobsson
- Gotham lamps
- Pablo Picasso *Ramie 375*
- Picasso ceramic *Madoura* 1956 plate

- Roberto Cavalli clothing
- Chanel couture clothing
- Geoffrey D. Harcourt lounge chair
- Hermès handbags and bracelet
- Christian Louboutin clutch evening purse
- Versace clothing
- Givenchy clothing
- Tiffany & Co. jewelry
- Prada clothing
- Cartier jewelry

Furniture styles

- Abstract art
- Adirondack
- American classical
- Anglo-Indian
- Art deco
- Art nouveau
- Baroque
- Biedermeier
- Black Forest
- Colonial
- Empire
- Federal
- French provincial
- Georgian
- Gothic
- Gustavian
- Hepplewhite
- Industrial
- Jacobean
- Louis XIII, XIV, XV, XVI
- Mid-century modern
- Minimalist
- Napoleon III
- Native American
- Neoclassical and revival
- Queen Anne
- Regency
- Renaissance revival
- Rococo
- Scandinavian modern
- Spanish
- Victorian

Jewelry styles

- Art deco
- Art nouveau
- Contemporary
- Edwardian
- Georgian
- Modern

- Neoclassical
- Retro
- Revival
- Rococo
- Victorian

Fine-art styles

- Abstract
- Academic
- American modern
- Art deco
- Art nouveau
- Baroque
- Contemporary
- Cubist
- Dada

- Expressionist
- Folk art
- Impressionist
- Minimalist
- Modern
- Old Masters
- Pop art
- Realist
- Victorian

Rarely will family leave any expensive jewelry, but watch for it. When fine jewelry is left for a sale, I ask the family if I may take it to a local company who appraises fine jewelry, thus using local trend pricing. Generally, the family is very pleased that I take my time to do that for any and all small items. It really helps to find a local company that you've been referred to for their knowledge and expertise.

Chapter Twelve

WHAT DID IT SELL FOR?

During your business adventure, you'll come across literally hundreds of thousands of items you must research because they are out of the ordinary, needing current pricing for each. I'll share a few items that were out of the ordinary for me to give you an idea of what I'm talking about. Make sure to check online for current pricing when reading this guide. You'll be amazed at the fluctuation from month to month and year to year. Plus, once you begin, pay close attention to furniture purchase pricing. Antiques when I began in 1990 were off-the-wall high and now, at time of print, they've gone down 75 percent! Contemporary sleek lines are sought after by customers who are now feathering their nests. All or most baby boomers searched for Victorian solid wood furniture, but currently younger buyers want more modern and less expensive furniture. Of course, if the younger ones grew up learning about fine furniture as mine, they would seek finer pieces, either modern or vintage. It's all relative to what is in vogue at the time.

Have you ever wondered what something is worth or what that piece would sell for? Since I've been in the estate sales business for almost 30 years, I thought it appropriate to share my findings. So many people have wonderful items to sell and haven't a clue of what they're worth.

I've chosen a few items that are rarely seen that sold at my sales. Keep in mind as I divulge pricing, I handle estates in the Midwest, which oftentimes pale in comparison to the amounts finalized on the East and West Coasts. TV shows state various prices an item *should* bring at auction, but estate sales rarely bring what they profess. Therefore, throngs of persons attend sales throughout the country to *pick up* items generally at a fraction of the cost, then sell them online hoping to find that one bidder from around the world that wants their item at almost unheard of prices. These are but a few of the reasons to note pricing if you choose to sell your items as well.

PLASTIC VERSUS CELLULOID[1]: WHAT ARE THE DIFFERENCES?

Developed in the 1930s,[2] the clear acrylic plastic branded as Lucite became a wildly popular material for costume jewelry.[3] Less expensive to produce than Bakelite,[4] Galalith, and Catalin and more chemically stable than celluloid, Lucite made these earlier jewelry plastics obsolete.

"Patented in 1869, Celluloid was not the first man-made plastic—that honor goes to Parkesine, which was formulated in 1865 by a Birmingham, England, inventor named Alexander Parkes, who combined collodion (used in tintypes[5] and ambrotypes[6]), camphor, and vegetable oil so it could be rolled into sheets and adhered to cloth, making the resulting material waterproof. Unfortunately, Parkesine proved brittle and its key ingredient, collodion, was highly flammable. In his zeal to cut manufacturing costs, Parkes ended up producing a product of poor quality. The firm closed in 1868.

"Meanwhile, in the United States, an inventor named John Wesley Hyatt was experimenting with nitrocellulose, whose main ingredient is a plant fiber called cellulose and whose soluble form is collodion. Like Parkes, Hyatt was trying to create a plastic, but his sights were set on billiard balls—a company called Phelan & Colander had promised $10,000 to anyone who could come up with a substitute for ivory, which even in the 19th century was a dwindling resource. Hyatt did not win the prize, but in the course of trying to produce the ball, he noticed that when camphor was added to nitrocellulose, the combination plasticized. In 1868 and 1870 respectively, Hyatt formed the Albany Billiard Ball Company and the Albany Dental Plate Company to put his invention to work, but his main claim to fame was the Celluloid Manufacturing Company, which was founded in 1872 when the Dental Plate Company's name was changed.

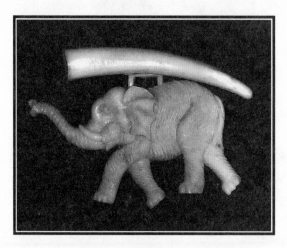

"For years, Celluloid could only be used in certain applications because of its flammability. . . . Celluloid-coated billiard balls would sometimes produce small explosions when they collided with each other. Similarly, the coating's use in movie film sparked countless fires in hot projection rooms. . . . [A] 'safety film' [was created] in 1900. A few years later, in 1907, Leo Baekeland created the first fully synthetic plastic, which he called Bakelite.[7]

"The advent of hard, carvable Bakelite and this new, somewhat-less-flammable version of celluloid ... spurred even more uses of the material, particularly in costume jewelry."

Both photos show items that were for sale on eBay. Once you get the hang of it, you'll know not only by the look of the piece but also by the feel of it. Celluloid is made of a sturdier, more solid feel and oftentimes is a bit colder to the touch. At least, that's my take on celluloid. Plastic is easier to detect since it's extremely prevalent at this time and it's generally less heavy with less attention to detail.

ATMOS CLOCKS[8]

The **Atmos atmosphere 1960s clock**[9] developed and made by Jaeger-LeCoultre, French master watchmakers, bears little resemblance to its 1760 predecessor mentioned below.

We sold this clock at an estate sale, as well as in 2008 for $225. I had it priced higher, but if you know the estate sale drill, bids are taken, from which the highest buys it, thus this ending price.

I sold yet another LeCoultre this year with the original box and in mint condition, which sold for $600. As always, it was the highest bidder and, better yet, sold at the current selling rate.

**Jaeger-LeCoultre
Geneve
Mantle clock**

I've had one of these treasures for at least 20 years now. When I purchased it at an estate, it came with the original instruction sheet.

The Atmos clock has been designed to run silently and with great accuracy indefinitely! No hand-winding, no electricity. Atmos is powered only by the changes in the temperature of the atmosphere around it! (Simply amazing!)

Perpetual energy was first discovered in 1760 when James Cox used the changes in atmospheric pressure as a motive force for a clock. This famous British horologist created an enormous, complicated, and costly instrument. It required 150 pounds of mercury to activate the mechanism! Because of its prodigious size, intricate design, and great expense, it immediately became a rare "curiosity" to be exhibited in museums ever since.

The round, golden box behind the mechanism contains a unique metal bellows that contracts and expands as the temperature rises and falls. This action is transmitted to the winding spring by the chain secured to the base of the bellows and wound around the barrel, winding the spring with every change of temperature. A change of only two degrees will wind your Atmos for 48 hours, even in air-conditioned rooms!

This reminds me of my father's ingenious attempt at creating a perpetual motion energy source for our personal homes. He never rendered it active, but he brilliantly went through the process even down to a mock-up energy source. Bravo, my lovely father!

These clocks are worth thousands of dollars when new, but one can purchase one via an estate sale or online for a cheaper price.

With the exception of the original Antique "Atmos I" and "Atmos II" (Mercury Reutter models), the following chart lists Atmos clocks[10] beginning with some of the earliest models (or calibers) and their respective serial numbers:

Caliber/Model	Serial Number	Approximate Year Manufactured
519	25,000–59,000	Late 1940s to 1950s
532	Unknown, identical to Model 522	Unknown, only a few manufactured
522	60,000–69,999	1950s
526-5	70,000–107,000	1950s
526-6, 528	107,007–599,999	1960–1980
540s	600,000 and up	1980–1998

HOW MUCH IS YOUR ATMOS CLOCK WORTH?

Determining the value of an Atmos Clock depends on the model, age, and overall condition of the clock, and the actual value can vary significantly depending on what the market will bear at that particular time.

The more common types of Atmos clocks have been trading at prices as low as $300 and as high as $1,200. These prices would be reflective of a typical Atmos clock, such as a model/caliber 519, 526, 528 and/or 540 and with the standard brass, gold-plated case.

Atmos clocks with oriental motif cases (white or black Plexiglas), the Gruen wood case models, or any other models with rare and unique cases would obviously be worth more than the types described above, depending on their condition.

There are numerous bits of information one can locate while perusing online information. However, to me, the best is to actually sell one or to own one. I realize the price we received enabled someone to sell it internationally, which is what this arena is all about.

I must add, I've owned mine for two decades now—good-ness, that sounds awfully long—and it works like a charm! I've never had to service it, nor has it ever stopped working.

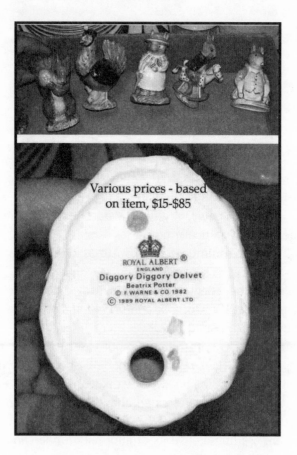

Hoiser cabinet sold for $125 Blue heater $60

Each sold for $20 to $30

Sold for
$125

Cranberry light

Sold
for
$700

Blue onion
lamp $145

Cat vases sold for $125 pair

vintage coffee grinder sold for $15

Shawnee bowls soldfor $15 set

Toby mugs sold for $50-$125 each

Royal Copenhagen dish set sold for $700. Retail was over $5000.

A good book to use as a guide is *300 Years of Kitchen Collectibles* by Linda Campbell Franklin. A few small items to look for: Depression, Fire-King, primitives, children's plates, crystal, and items made in Germany, such as plates, cups, steins, and glassware. Keep an eye out for working old clocks; nonworking will sell but not for as much. I can't stress this enough: *Look on the bottom of the items for names and markings.*

Precious Moments and Hummels are poor sellers right now. The past few years Noritake and Mikasa china plate sets and those from Occupied Japan often sell. These Occupied Japan items were made when General MacArthur and troops were occupying Japan for a few years during World War II. So many things have changed from 1989 when I began—antiques to date have dropped 70 to 75 percent in sales!

Baby boomers were enthralled with antiques, buying them by the dozens, refinishing them to their original splendor. Now baby boomers are selling these items at greatly reduced prices, and those who are buying are the younger crowd, 40 and younger.

When a trend changes, and they always do, it's very wise to inform your clients of such so they won't have a *sticker shock* reaction after noting your pricing.

Doilies also are sought after, so learn about their pricing from other sales.

Dolls can also be a very good item! This Jumeau[11] automaton doll is very unique!

An example of what they sold for in the past 15 years is this 18-inch German character boy doll, dating from the early 1900s, which sold in the early 2000s for $3,100. Now it's gone down to an asking price of under $1,000. The appraised value in 2010 of a Jumeau automaton, ca. 1900, on the *Antiques Roadshow* was $30,999 to $35,000. These were sold via a few of the larger auction houses throughout the country.

Jumeau Doll Mark Identification

Some Jumeau dolls are only marked with a **size number** on the back of the head and a red or blue Jumeau mark on the body.

Jumeau Medaille d'Or Paris	Déposé Tete Jumeau Bte SGDG [Size number]	Bébé Français BG. F	Déposé Tete Jumeau	E. J. A	E. 8D.
Bébé Jumeau Diplôme d'Honneur	Brevete SGDG	Déposé Tete Jumeau Bte SGDG	Déposé E. 7 J.	8 E J	E. 9J.
Jumeau Paris	Bébé Jumeau Déposé	Déposé Jumeau [Size number]	V [big, open checkmark]	Déposé Jumeau [Size number]	E. Déposé J
B. 12 L.	214 Déposé Jumeau Bte SGDG Unis France	306 Jumeau 1938 Paris	1907	1907 Tete Jumeau	Paris [bee symbol] Déposé

** **SGDG** = Sans Garantie Du Gouvernement—a registered patent without government guarantee.

Bisque doll heads marked **10731 Mirette** (by Gebruder Heubach) have been found on marked Jumeau bodies.

Bébé Bon Marche, Bébé Trois Quartiers, Louvre Bébé, and Bébé Samaritaine are all attributed to Jumeau.

HAMILTON BABY GRAND MADE BY BALDWIN

Factory location: Loveland, Ohio; Serial Number Dates: 1890–Present

History: Established in 1862, the Baldwin Piano Company continues to be one of the major American manufacturers of grand and baby grand pianos. The Baldwin Company also made Hamilton, Howard Ellington, Valley Gem, Saint Regis, Schroeder, Franke, Acrosonic, Kremlin, Modello, Monarch, Sargent, and Winton pianos.

Our piano sold for $600 in 2009, which wasn't much, but with the proliferation of small electronic keyboards, pianos are hard to sell. Anytime a family member or friend purchases something like this, the price is always a bit higher than a customer off the street.

Remember these sellers had to find, with my help, someone who really wanted it, and we found that person! With proper advertisement, photos, and a good following of clients, the word went out, which created the "stir" that brings in the potential buyer.

The Hamilton Organ Company began in 1889, which became the Baldwin Piano Company the following year. The company, now a subsidiary of Gibson Guitar Corporation, has manufactured instruments under the Baldwin, Chickering, Wurlitzer, Hamilton, and Howard names.

Of course, the list of items could be endless. You'll soon have a list of items that you *thought* would have brought one price, and yet have it bring in so much more by utilizing the process of bidding!

Tiger & cub
Korea' hollow BRONZE
Teakwood base   (this has been in the family since early 40's)

One example is a kind, sweet lady named Susie who commissioned a sale for me to handle. Within her ranch home, she directed me to the basement to view a hollow, bronze, large figurine, stating it had been in the family since the 1940s. Friends told her it should be worth $50,000! I wasn't sure about that exorbitant figure and said I'd research it and let her know.

The inscription read "made in Korea." So I began my research. It took me quite a bit of time to find anything similar to it, much less a match. What the research showed was various figures made in Korea and a vast array of prices all over the board.

I told Susie my findings and suggested I place a notice online and on the figure that we are taking bids on it in order to bring the best price. She agreed. When the sale began, she told me it just had to go and that she'd take $500 if I could get it.

A couple of my co-workers carried it upstairs, where we prominently displayed it. I made a sign stating bids would be taken at the cashier's table. Within two hours, a man walked in, checked it out, and left a bid of $2,350. When I saw the bid, the handwriting was shaky, so I asked if I had the correct amount. The man said *yes*, asking when he'd find out if he was the highest bidder. I told him I'd call him or the highest bidder by 5 P.M. that evening.

It turned out he was the highest bidder and, in fact, the only bidder! I called him as promised, and he paid for it and picked it up the following day.

Susie was at the house the following morning since she still lived there. Before we opened the doors for the sale, I told her the highest bidder was to pay $2,350 for the tiger. She wept tears of joy! She told me that something happened with the plumbing last week, and she had to pay out $2,000. Now she'd recoup what she spent.

She thanked and thanked me for helping her sell that tiger for a decent amount.

Chapter Thirteen

HOW TO BUILD YOUR CUSTOMER BASE AND KEEP IT!

"The foundational stones for a balanced success are honesty, character, integrity, faith, love and loyalty."

— ZIG ZIGLAR

"When you are able to maintain your own highest standards of integrity—regardless of what others may do—you are destined for greatness."

— NAPOLEON HILL

At all my sales, I'm the one taking the money, answering questions, and directing workers to help buyers with this or that. But the most important gift I give to my customers is truthfulness.

Many customers hug me when they enter the estate. Goodness, I never knew this business could be so sweet!

Customers who return over and over to my sales have told me it's because of my constant honesty and kindness. I know my upbringing was right on! Dad taught us to say what we mean and mean what we say. He, too, had his own company, a barbershop filled with loyal customers.

These are my golden rules!

First and foremost, be *truthful*. You'll never succeed in a business if you lie.

Second, be *kind* to one and all. Sure, you'll have to stand up to some, but if you're sincere and show kindness, you'll win over even the haughtiest of persons.

Third, be *considerate*. Clients call because they've lost a loved one, which means they're still in a grieving mode. Don't hurt their feelings more. Be compassionate.

Fourth, be *calm*. Clients are generally in a tizzy about what to do next. Staying calm yourself helps the clients become and stay calm.

Utilize the golden rule: **"do unto others as you would have them do unto you."** In other words, treat others as you'd like to be treated.

So often customers enter my sales with a smile, stating they'd just been to an estate sale where the commissioned estate sale personnel were rude to one and all. Over the years, they state time and again how glad they are that I'm consistently kind to everyone.

I use their testimonials as references when a new client requests them.

One example of a referral from a sale in Florissant was:

We received the package yesterday with the checks and the listings of sales. We appreciate all the effort you put into the estate sale. What a process!! Thanks, again, for all you did! Was great meeting and visiting with you.
Take care, wishing you all the best!

Mrs. A

With a sale in Creve Coeur, when I called the client to verify he had received the list of items sold and the check, Mr. S said, "Yes, Victoria, I got it. I must say you're a very honorable woman. A very honorable woman."

After I sent another client their check, the wife called for my address and sent a $300 bonus! I've never received a bonus in this form!

One of my clients, Ms. B, lived in California while her brother was on the East Coast. Both had little time to travel back and forth. She found me online, checked out my references, flew to St. Louis, and liked me instantly! She signed the contract with her brother present, turned over the key after she and her brother gathered a few mementos, and left to their respective homes. I sold all the items with only a few remainder items left over. Over the phone, Ms. B said she couldn't have done it without me and had to be out before her sister's next month's rent came due. We made it just in time.

A client named Mrs. M sent this e-mail:

> *Hello Victoria:*
>
> *You were recommended to me by a realtor, Mrs. M. I am helping my dad prepare to sell his home. He recently moved into a retirement apartment. I live in the Kansas City area. The house is in St. Charles, MO. If you need to come by to see it, I can arrange for my Dad, a friend, or the realtor to meet you there. My hope is to perhaps have the sale in mid- to late June.*

We did the sale in late June and, to her amazement, most of the items sold! The realtor and she were both pleased. She came by the weekend of the sale and thanked me for pulling it together so quickly and efficiently. She was astonished at the items long ago forgotten that we pulled out from various boxes and closets.

The realtor now often sends me similar requests.

And lastly, from the referral sale mentioned above:

> **To:** *Victoria Gray*
>
> **Subject:** *Re: Update on total sales*
>
> *WOW!!!! That is amazing!!!*
>
> *Victoria, I know that I told you this yesterday, but I want to repeat it again. You have been such a blessing to our family during some incredibly difficult times. Dad is certainly smiling down on you and blessing your*

continued successes.

YOU ROCK!!!!!! Thanks again, Mrs. J

And then her sister:

To: *Victoria Gray*

Subject: *Re: Update on total sales*

I second J's comments! Thank you VERY MUCH!!!! Mother was VERY pleased with the results and we are all very thankful the piano sold! WOO HOO!!

Sincerely, Mrs. S

I'd met the father just two weeks before he died. There were several adult children from this marriage. All were so tickled that so many items sold. This sale housed a ton of vintage patterns. We sold over a hundred at $4 each! They thought no one would even want the patterns. But guess what? Vintage patterns from the '40s to the '80s are sought after at present.

This is what you want: pleased clients and pleased realtors that refer new clients periodically throughout the years.

So go out there! Start your new business or just handle your relative's sale yourself!

You can do it! If I can do it as a widow with four kids, anyone can surely be successful, too!

RESOURCES

Hay House Alaskan cruise/Movers & Shakers seminars

Movers & Shakers guidebook

Cheryl Richardson—coach on Movers & Shakers cruise

Reid Tracy—Hay House CEO and coach on Movers & Shakers cruise

Platform: Get Noticed in a Noisy World by Michael Hyatt

Jeff Walker—How to Not Suck on Video—http://jeffwalker .com/how-to-not-suck-on-video

WordPress.com

www.victoriagray.net

www.lawyers.com

www.blogger.com

www.godaddy.com

www.vistaprint.com

www.storesupply.com

www.signsonthecheap.com

www.estatesales.net

www.linkedin.com

www.craigslist.org

www.bakelitemuseum.net

www.1stdibs.com

ENDNOTES

Chapter 1

1. https://www.sos.mo.gov/business/outreach/starting_steps
2. https://www.score.org

Chapter 5

1. www.signsonthecheap.com
2. www.storesupply.com

Chapter 6

1. https://alwaystreasured.com/
   the-most-collectible-names-in-vintage-costume-jewelry

2. https://alwaystreasured.com/
   the-most-collectible-names-in-vintage-costume-jewelry

3. http://paranormal.lovetoknow.com/Ghost_Orbs_Different_Colors

4. http://paranormal.lovetoknow.com/Ghost_Orbs_Different_Colors

5. http://newthoughtlibrary.com/shinnFlorenceScovel/game/#prosperity

6. http://www.paranormal-encounters.com/wp/
   do-our-pets-visit-us-after-death

Chapter 7

1. http://www.builtstlouis.net/arena01.html

Chapter 8

1. http://theankleexpress.com

Chapter 11

1. www.1stdibs.com

Chapter 12

1. http://www.collectorsweekly.com/costume-jewelry/celluloid
2. http://www.collectorsweekly.com/1930s
3. http://www.collectorsweekly.com/costume-jewelry/overview
4. http://www.collectorsweekly.com/costume-jewelry/bakelite
5. http://www.collectorsweekly.com/photographs/tintypes
6. http://www.collectorsweekly.com/photographs/ambrotypes
7. http://www.collectorsweekly.com/costume-jewelry/bakelite
8. http://www.atmosclocks.com/history.html
9. http://www.atmosclocks.com/dating.html
10. http://www.pbs.org/wgbh/roadshow/season/15/washington-dc/appraisals/jumeau-automaton-ca-1900--201006A31
11. http://dollreference.com/jumeau_bebes_dolls_france.html
12. https://en.wikipedia.org/wiki/Baldwin_Piano_Company

ACKNOWLEDGMENTS

I'd like to posthumously acknowledge my father for his continued loving kindness and day-to-day support.

ABOUT THE AUTHOR

Victoria Gray, a widow with four grown adult children, lives in St. Louis, Missouri. She owned and operated Pro-Q Auction and Estate Sales Company for 10 years, after which she began her full-fledged Estate Sales by Victoria business in 1999. Her areas of appraisal competence include antiques, furniture, art, collectibles, glassware, jewelry, figurines, pottery, toys, and depreciating residential contents.

She has held various positions, such as a public speaker of historical fashion shows via Designs and Creations by Victoria (2005–2014), vice president of the St. Louis Writers Guild, and art director for Wentworth Art Galleries. While an art director, she gained knowledge of contemporary artists and traveled to Sweden for an art education course. Victoria owned an antiquities and collectibles store and a design store called Quilts Etc. She is an apt seamstress, and customers of a local Laura Ashley store hired her to decorate, design, and create such items as window treatments, slip covers, and quilts.

Sipping a cup of her favorite English tea, Victoria journals every morning as the sun comes up. New books are created within her 70 journals to date, such as *The Secret of a Widow's Vision: The Vision from Within*, *Life after Life with Dad*, Detective Q Mysteries series, *My Sister's Salvation*, and more.

Hay House Titles of Related Interest

YOU CAN HEAL YOUR LIFE, the movie,
starring Louise Hay & Friends
(available as a 1-DVD program, an expanded 2-DVD set,
and an online streaming video)
Learn more at www.hayhouse.com/louise-movie

THE SHIFT, the movie,
starring Dr. Wayne W. Dyer
(available as a 1-DVD program, an expanded 2-DVD set,
and an online streaming video)
Learn more at www.hayhouse.com/the-shift-movie

*WHAT YOUR CLUTTER IS TRYING TO TELL YOU: Uncover the
Message in the Mess and Reclaim Your Life,* by Kerri Richardson

All of the above are available at your local bookstore,
or may be ordered by contacting Hay House (see next page).

We hope you enjoyed this Hay House book. If you'd like to receive our online catalog featuring additional information on Hay House books and products, or if you'd like to find out more about the Hay Foundation, please contact:

Hay House, Inc., P.O. Box 5100, Carlsbad, CA 92018-5100
(760) 431-7695 or (800) 654-5126
(760) 431-6948 (fax) or (800) 650-5115 (fax)
www.hayhouse.com® • www.hayfoundation.org

Published and distributed in Australia by:
Hay House Australia Pty. Ltd., 18/36 Ralph St., Alexandria NSW 2015
Phone: 612-9669-4299 • *Fax:* 612-9669-4144 • www.hayhouse.com.au

Published and distributed in the United Kingdom by:
Hay House UK, Ltd., Astley House, 33 Notting Hill Gate, London W11 3JQ
Phone: 44-20-3675-2450 • *Fax:* 44-20-3675-2451 • www.hayhouse.co.uk

Published and distributed in the Republic of South Africa by:
Hay House SA (Pty), Ltd., P.O. Box 990, Witkoppen 2068
info@hayhouse.co.za • www.hayhouse.co.za

Published in India by: Hay House Publishers India,
Muskaan Complex, Plot No. 3, B-2, Vasant Kunj, New Delhi 110 070
Phone: 91-11-4176-1620 • *Fax:* 91-11-4176-1630 • www.hayhouse.co.in

Distributed in Canada by:
Raincoast Books, 2440 Viking Way, Richmond, B.C. V6V 1N2
Phone: 1-800-663-5714 • *Fax:* 1-800-565-3770 • www.raincoast.com

ACCESS NEW KNOWLEDGE.
ANYTIME. ANYWHERE.

Learn and evolve at your own pace with the world's leading experts.

www.hayhouseU.com

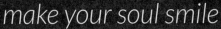